THE MODERN STATE

THE MODERN STATE

by

LEONARD WOOLF
LORD EUSTACE PERCY
MRS. SIDNEY WEBB
PROFESSOR W. G. S. ADAMS
SIR ARTHUR SALTER

edited by
MARY ADAMS

KENNIKAT PRESS, INC./PORT WASHINGTON, N. Y.

THE MODERN STATE

First published 1933
Reissued 1969 by Kennikat Press

Library of Congress Catalog Card No: 68-26225
Manufactured in the United States of America

ESSAY AND GENERAL LITERATURE INDEX REPRINT SERIES

EDITOR'S FOREWORD

THIS book is based on a series of broadcast talks on political and social theory which formed part of a comprehensive symposium on *The Changing World*.

The purpose of the talks was to reveal the quick succession of changes which have taken place in the modern State since the beginning of the century, and to direct attention to those developments in nineteenth-century political thought and social practice of which those changes were the direct consequence.

Mr. Leonard Woolf and Lord Eustace Percy in Part I discuss developments in the idea of democracy and argue the case for its survival in the world to-day.

In Part II Mrs. Sidney Webb describes some of the diseases of organised society—those forces of herd behaviour which injure the commonwealth by their exclusiveness, their callousness, or their willlessness; and Professor W. G. S. Adams examines the qualities and defects of Parliamentary Government, concluding that this representative order is still the best form of government which has been devised.

The problem of world order is the subject of Part III, and here Sir Arthur Salter examines the riddle of the world's two great needs—peace and prosperity.

Changes have been made here and there in the form in which these talks appeared, changes for which the editor is responsible. But the talks are mostly published as they were delivered, and still retain that informality of style which often illuminates broadcasting. It is not unnatural that the authors should feel a certain uneasiness at the publication of material which, in a longer book, they might have wished to qualify with explanations and reservations, and the note with which Mr. Woolf has prudently prefaced his section might well be held to represent the point of view of the other contributors.

The talks were arranged under the auspices of the Central Council for Broadcast Adult Education, and the courtesy of the British Broadcasting Corporation in giving permission for their publication is acknowledged.

M. A.

January 1933

CONTENTS

PART III

WORLD GOVERNMENT

by Sir Arthur Salter

CONTRIBUTORS

PROFESSOR W. G. S. ADAMS (Fellow of All Souls College, Oxford, and Gladstone Professor of Political Theory and Institutions at Oxford).

LORD EUSTACE PERCY (President of the Board of Education, 1924–29, author of *Democracy on Trial*, etc.).

SIR ARTHUR SALTER, K.C.B. (Director, Economic and Finance Section, League of Nations, 1922–30. General Secretary Reparations Commission, 1920–22, author of *Allied Shipping Control: An Experiment in International Administration* and *Recovery*).

MRS. SIDNEY WEBB (Fellow of the British Academy; author, jointly with her husband, of works on Trade Unionism, Co-operation and English Local Government).

LEONARD WOOLF (Founder of the Hogarth Press and Literary Editor of the *Nation* until 1930, author of *After the Deluge, Economic Imperialism*, etc.).

PART I

CAN DEMOCRACY SURVIVE?

LEONARD WOOLF

and

LORD EUSTACE PERCY

LEONARD WOOLF

1. WHAT IS DEMOCRACY?

[*It is with great hesitation that I have agreed to the reprinting of these six talks. It is impossible in a half-hour talk to put in the explanations and reservations one would make if treating the subject connectedly in book form. The view given, therefore, when these talks are collected and reprinted, is necessarily one-sided and incomplete.*]

No one can doubt that the world has changed enormously in the last thirty or fifty years. The country and the society in which you and I are living to-day is completely different from that in which our grandfathers and even our fathers lived. The changes which I shall be discussing are the political changes, and I shall therefore have to talk to you a good deal about political ideas, about what is going on inside people's heads. For these are the really important political changes. The most important things from the political and social point of view are not constitutions and Acts of Parliament; they are not General Elections or the ups and downs of political parties; they are the changes which take place in our ideas, in the ideas of ordinary people as to what Kings and Governments, Railway Companies or Trade Unions ought to do, and in the ideas of Kings and Cabinet Ministers and Civil

Servants, of Railway Directors and Trade Union Leaders with regard to their duties towards the public.

I believe that what goes on inside people's heads is much more important in every department of life than most people think, but politically it is peculiarly important. The discovery of gold in one part of the world or the migration of herrings from one part of the ocean to another may cause a revolution in the economic life of Europe. That is the kind of concrete change which hardly ever occurs in politics. Compare it for a moment with the political revolution which we have all seen in our own lifetime, the emancipation of women. To-day women have the same political status as men, they are M.P.s, Cabinet Ministers, doctors, lawyers. They can, if they choose, live the same kind of life that men live. But that was not the case in 1900. This revolution is the result of a change in political and social ideas. First, large numbers of women began to think that they ought to have equal political rights with men and the opportunity of entering men's professions and occupations, and then they convinced large numbers of men of the rightness and justice of the claim. The revolution was made possible only by the change inside our own heads.

I want to begin by putting all my cards on the table. My view is that the most important political changes which have taken place since 1900 are concerned with the ideas of what we call democracy.

They are largely the result of a struggle or conflict between democracy and ideas which are contrary or hostile to democracy. You will see this in a general way if you try to imagine the political landscape of Europe in 1900 and compare it with the same political landscape to-day. In 1900 nearly everyone would have said that they were living in a democratic age, and that the government and society of practically every European country were getting more and more democratic. It is true that many countries which are now republics were in 1900 monarchies, but most of the kings were constitutional monarchs and would have been proud to be called the democratic head of a great democracy.

That brings me to my second point, namely, that in the first ten years of the twentieth century nearly everyone believed, or pretended to believe, in democracy. Kings, Conservatives, Liberals, and Socialists—all professed to be democrats. The difference between them was not as to whether democracy was or was not a good thing; they differed mainly about how quickly it was safe to establish democracy. In 1900 if you thought that it was only safe to establish democracy slowly, you called yourself a Conservative; if you thought it safe to establish democracy quickly, you called yourself a Liberal; but whether you called yourself the one or the other, you both professed to believe in the blessings of democracy.

And it is worth pointing out that this in itself was a very new thing. If you read the letters of Queen Victoria or the life of a statesman like Lord Salisbury, you will see that only twenty years before 1900, in the eighteen eighties, democracy was still hardly respectable. At any rate, the Queen herself, the Conservative leaders, and many of the Liberal leaders thought democracy extremely dangerous and were openly opposed to it. In those days Sir Charles Dilke and Joseph Chamberlain were regarded by the Queen and the Conservatives as a kind of dangerous Bolshevik because they stood openly for democracy. Twenty-five years later, say in 1905, the whole situation had completely altered and the King and the Conservative Party had accepted democracy as safe and inevitable. How deep the change had been can be seen best if you compare the attitude of Lord Salisbury towards democracy with that of the two Conservative Prime Ministers who followed him—Lord Balfour and Mr. Bonar Law. The ideas and the policy of these two Prime Ministers were not a bit less democratic than had been those of Sir Charles Dilke and Mr. Chamberlain.

The political landscape in 1900 was, then, thoroughly democratic. Everyone believed in democracy; most people believed that democracy was already successful and established, and that civilized countries would go on getting more and more democratic. But in the last thirty years there has been another change and the political landscape is now quite different. The change has taken place both in the position of democracy and in the attitude of people towards it.

Think for a moment first of the facts themselves. The war, which ended only thirteen years ago, was fought by the Allies on behalf of democracy, in order, as we said, to make the world safe for democracy. But no one can say to-day that the world is safe for democracy in many countries of Europe. During the last ten years at one time or another we have seen democratic government entirely abolished and dictatorships established in Russia, Italy, Spain, Poland, Hungary, Bulgaria, and Greece. In Germany and Austria constitutional government has been continually threatened by Fascists on the right and Communists on the left, and in either of these countries a dictatorship might be successfully established at any moment. I want you to realize exactly what that means. It means that in the last decade half the population of Europe have been governed by dictatorships, and that over 60 per cent of the population have been living in countries in which democracy has either been completely abolished or has been in deadly peril.

It is surely a strange fact that immediately after the Allies had successfully fought a war which was to make the world safe for democracy, nearly three-quarters of the people of Europe should find democratic government destroyed or in danger of destruction in their own countries. But this change has taken place not only in the Governments under which people live; it has also taken place inside their own heads, in their political ideas.

It is a very interesting thing to observe the changes that have taken place during the last fifty years in the general attitude of Europeans towards democratic government. At the beginning of the period, those on the Right in politics, the aristocracies and Conservative parties, were still very much opposed to democracy; they feared it, thinking that the establishment of full democratic government would mean the establishment of mob rule and the breakdown of law and order. Lord Salisbury and the Queen in England, Bismarck and the old Emperor William in Germany, the monarchists and the parties of the Right in France, and all Russian statesmen held these views. Twenty-five years later this opposition to democracy and the fear of it had practically died out, and everyone, except a very few old-fashioned people, believed, or thought they believed, in democracy. And now in the next twenty-five years this change has gone still further and a very strange thing has happened. To-day the Conservatives and those on the Right in politics have not only completely lost their fear of it; they are either among its chief supporters or they simply despise it. On the other hand, it is on the extreme Left that you will find many of the most bitter opponents of democratic government. This is not an exaggeration or a paradox; it is merely the bare truth, as you will find if you think for a moment about the facts. The most bitter opponents of democracy are Communists, but most Communists, if they had lived fifty years ago, would have been radicals and democrats. One of the chief charges which many Conservatives bring against Communist Governments is that they destroy democracy and establish a dictatorship—and many of these Conservatives, had they lived fifty years ago, would have feared and opposed democracy. Fascists, again, simply despise democracy, believing it to be a hopelessly weak and inefficient form of government; fifty years ago they too would not have despised but have feared it.

Democracy is indeed a bit out of fashion and out of favour. Those who opposed and feared it have lost their fear of it, partly because they think that it will not produce those results which they anticipated. Those who were enthusiastic for it have lost their enthusiasm, perhaps for the same reason. At any rate you have only to look at one of the political monthly or weekly papers or to read a serious book on politics, and you will see that there is a general feeling that democracy has failed or is failing.

It is easy to give actual concrete examples of this feeling. For instance, twenty-five years ago parliamentary government was regarded almost universally as the essence of democracy. To-day in our own country you may often see statements implying that parliamentary government is not working. Parliament, it is said, is impotent and is called a "talking-shop" or some other contemptuous name; or we are told that all power is falling into the hands of a bureaucracy, the Civil Service, and that the people have no power over their Governments. And on the Continent these views are even more general and more violent. In many European countries, which established parliamentary government more or less on the English model, the system never worked as smoothly as here, and even before the rise of the dictatorships there was considerable dissatisfaction with the way it worked. This is certainly true of a country like Italy, and there people's dissatisfaction with the working of the parliamentary system led to a general feeling of disappointment with democracy, and so may be said to have helped to pave the way to the Fascist dictatorship.

I think that perhaps these examples are sufficient to show you the kind of way in which opposition to and disappointment with democracy have been working in recent years. At the same time I do not want to give you a one-sided view of the picture. You must not think that all forces have been against democracy. No, all the time that this opposition to democracy has been growing, democracy itself and democratic government have been growing and expanding too. Remember that universal suffrage and women's suffrage have been established in this and other countries only a very few years ago, and these are advanced forms of democratic government. Remember that although a dictatorship was established for some time in Spain, it has been followed by a republic and a more democratic type of government than that country has ever previously enjoyed. Remember, too, that, though the Nazis threaten the German Government on one side with a dictatorship and the Communists threaten on the other, the actual government of Germany and its constitution has been ever since the war infinitely more democratic than it was before the war.

You cannot really understand the changes which have taken place in politics during the last thirty years unless you also understand what democracy means.

The first thing to notice about democracy is that it rests on a new idea about happiness and particularly the happiness of ordinary people. The early democrats insisted that the day-to-day happiness of ordinary persons was immensely important. They maintained that the principal object of all government and Governments ought simply to be the happiness of the population. And they went on to assert that everyone has an equal right to the same kind of happiness.

This idea may seem to you so obvious and simple that it must be unimportant. It is really of immense importance. It was completely revolutionary when it was first put forward in the eighteenth century.

It was the foundation of the French Revolution, of democracy, and all democratic Governments. No one before the American and French Revolutions had believed that the principal object of a Government should be the happiness of all classes and all individuals. In the sixteenth century, for instance, most Governments considered that their main duty was not to see that their subjects were prosperous and happy, but to see that they believed certain religious beliefs. Again, before the birth of democracy it was always considered that the chief object of government was not to make ordinary people happy, but to maintain a system in which special classes had certain rights and privileges. In France in the eighteenth century the happiness of the peasants had no political importance compared with the rights of the nobility to hunt and keep pigeons. Before the nineteenth century practically no one in England thought that the son of a town or agricultural labourer had politically the right to enjoy the same kind of things and the same kind of happiness as the son of an aristocrat or a landed gentleman.

Wherever you have a system of government which is undemocratic or people whose ideas are hostile to democracy, you will find that they either openly or covertly deny that the equal happiness of all classes should be the chief concern of politics and Governments. Thus the militarist Governments of Germany and Russia before the war, which were anti-democratic, governed those countries on the principle that national power and prestige, military glory, and the privileges of the military and aristocratic classes were much more important than the everyday happiness of peasants and workers in factories. And to-day the Fascist and the Communist, both equally opposed to democracy, maintain that everything, including the happiness of the people, should be subordinated by the Government to the Fascist or Communist State, or to the systems of Fascism or Communism.

And finally consider this fact as an example. Every democrat would maintain that in a democratic country the happiness of everyone should be treated as of equal importance politically; that is to say, the Government should treat the happiness of all persons and classes—Conservatives, Liberals, Socialists, even the opponents of democracy —as equally important. But the Communist holds that the Government should treat the happiness of the bourgeois classes as of no importance at all, and the Fascist acts on the principle that the happiness of those who are not Fascists is of no importance to a Fascist Government.

The second idea underlying democracy is perhaps a little more difficult to understand. The essence of a democratic system of Government is that it treats everyone politically merely as an individual. Before the nineteenth century and the advent of democratic ideas no Government ever did that.

If you had been born in 1750, your position in society would have been definitely settled for you by your class and your birth. But what was even more important was that in those days any political rights or power that you might have had would have depended solely upon the fact that you were the son of your father, or that you belonged to a certain class, or owned certain property. For instance, if you belonged to some classes or were the son of a labourer, a shopkeeper, or a lawyer, you had no political power at all or any right to vote or take an active part in politics, but if you were the eldest son of a peer, you would eventually take your seat in the House of Lords; if you were the son of a landed gentleman you would have a good chance of sitting in the House of Commons; and if you owned certain pieces of landed property, you controlled so many votes.

This, you will notice, is just like the Fascist and the Communist systems; the Fascist Government gives a man political rights and powers if he is a Fascist which it refuses to the man who is not a Fascist, while the Communist Government treats a man politically as quite different according as he is a member of the Communist Party, a worker, or a middle-class man. On the other hand, the more democratic a country is, the more rigorously does the Government ignore all distinctions of class and property so far as a man's political rights are concerned. In the most democratic countries a man's right to vote or to take part in politics is determined solely by the fact that he is an individual. If one wants to put this very important distinction into a few words, one may say that democracy treats every man and woman politically simply as an individual and as an equal political unit; non-democratic systems treat people not as individuals but as members of different classes and give them different political rights because they are born in different classes, pursue different occupations, or hold different political views. These, then, are some of the broad changes which have taken place in our political ideas and therefore in politics and society.

2. HAPPINESS

IF you ever asked yourself the direct question: "Have I politically a right to be happy, and is it the duty of the Government to see that I have the same chance as other people of being happy?" I feel pretty certain that you would answer emphatically "Yes." It is, however, a curious fact that, if you had lived at any period before the nineteenth century, unless you had happened to belong to a very small privileged class of aristocrats, you would almost certainly have answered the same question with an emphatic "No." This change—one of the most important and disturbing of all the political and social changes in history—is the result of democracy.

The democratic ideal of happiness is so simple that you might easily underrate its importance. The very first democrats, the inventors of modern democracy, were the leaders in the American Revolution. In the Declaration of Independence, which is a kind of creed of the democratic faith, they told the world that the pursuit of happiness is an inalienable right of all men and that the object of government is to secure that right to all men. This idea, apparently so simple, is really extraordinarily revolutionary. If it were put into practice, the Government of every country would be carried on on the principle that the everyday happiness of ordinary people— that is, of the whole population—is by far the most important care of the Government, and, further, that every man and woman ought to be given, so far as possible, a chance of enjoying the same kind of happiness.

Now no Government except a democratic Government has ever tried to govern on that principle, and no Government since the beginning of the world has ever put it completely into practice. That alone shows how important and revolutionary this principle is.

The best way of understanding the meaning and importance of this principle is to observe how as a matter of fact many of the great political changes of recent times have been due to an attempt to put it into practice. Let me give you one or two examples. You all know that during the last fifty years or more some of the greatest political changes in this country, and indeed in nearly all European countries, have been connected with what is called social reform. Laws have been made regulating conditions of labour, limiting the number of hours which people may be required to work, making it compulsory to give employees one half-holiday every week, fixing minimum wages. Other laws have been made providing what are called social services— health and maternity services; better houses, drainage, lighting, trams; insurance; free libraries; recreation grounds and playing fields. Then again there is all the legislation which has provided universal education.

All this kind of legislation is recognized as being the result of democracy; it is essentially democratic legislation. It began, of course, before 1900, but the whole movement to provide all ordinary people with social services has enormously increased and strengthened during the last thirty years. And it is the direct result of the democratic idea that politically the everyday happiness of ordinary men and women is of the greatest importance, and that the first object of the State or the municipality or the Government should be to see that everyone has, so far as possible, an equal chance of this kind of happiness.

Take education as an example and examine it from this point of view. The democrat would argue in this way about education: he would say that the happiness of a person depends enormously upon the kind of education which he receives when a child or young person. It will not only determine whether he is capable of becoming a manual worker, a clerical worker, or a professional man; even more important, it will determine for him the kind of things he can understand and enjoy; for instance, a man who has never been taught to read would be obviously cut off from a large amount of happiness. The democrat maintains, therefore, that it is one of the first duties of a Government to provide universal education, and he would also maintain that in a really democratic country the Government ought to see that every child, no matter what class he was born in, had an equal opportunity of getting the best kind of education.

And now let us turn and see how the growth of this democratic view has actually caused political changes with regard to education. I am going to take you first right back to the beginning of the nineteenth century, to the time when democracy was just beginning. At that time a Bill was unsuccessfully introduced in the House of Commons for establishing elementary schools. It was opposed by the President of the Royal Society, Davies Giddy, who maintained that to give education "to the labouring classes of the poor" would be to "teach them to despise their lot in life, instead of making them good servants of agriculture and other laborious employments to which their rank in society had destined them." That was in 1807, and in those days, as you see, people still held the non-democratic view that the Government ought not to give the working classes the happiness which might come from education, because it might at the same time make them discontented with poverty and subordination. If you look forward from this date 1807 to 1850, the middle of the nineteenth century, you find that still in England large numbers of the population received no education at all and the Government did nothing to provide it for the less wealthy classes. In that year the total public expenditure on education was only £153,000. And now take another step forward to the year 1900. By that time the democratic view had made great progress; public elementary schools and universal education had been established, and public expenditure on education had risen from £150,000 to £27,000,000. But even in 1900 practically nothing beyond elementary education was provided by the State for the children of the great mass of the people, and the educational opportunities of the wealthy were much greater than those of other classes. And now, if you consider the period between 1900 and 1930, you will see that the democratic movement with regard to education made still further progress. No real democrat would be contented with the present position, for it is certainly not true in this country that every child has an equal opportunity of obtaining the maximum happiness from a good education. But something has been done to improve the schools and elementary education; to increase the opportunities of all children of going on from elementary to secondary and university education. Something has been done, too, towards raising the school-leaving age. And, finally, the public expenditure on education has been increased between 300 and 400 per cent during the last thirty years.

You will see from all this that the democratic view about happiness has had and is still having great effect upon such an important part of our lives as education. I want to give you one or two other similar examples. In 1850, which is not so very long ago, for there are a good many people

still living who were alive then—in 1850 the Government or the State did practically nothing to
ensure that the great mass of people were even
moderately happy. I read the other day a book
written in that year describing the appalling conditions of what were called the Rookeries, the tene-
ments in which the poor lived just off the Tottenham
Court Road. For instance, these people could only
get water for washing, cooking, and drinking on
two days out of every week and then the amount
that they got was very small. It was just the same
with all other things which we regard to-day not
as comforts but necessaries of life.

In the next fifty years the democratic view began
to prevail—that it was the duty of the State to see
that the whole population, poor as well as rich, was
provided with what we now regard as the bare
necessaries of a comfortable existence. By 1900 the
State or the municipality did provide most of those
bare necessaries, such as clean streets, water, light.
But in the last thirty years this movement, like that
of education, has gone much further. To-day the
State, and still more often municipalities, act on
the more advanced democratic view; they not only
provide necessaries, but try to provide means for
the mass of the population to enjoy itself.

I will give you only two examples, one big and
the other which may seem to you a small one. The
B.B.C. is what is called a Public Corporation, and
a Cabinet Minister, the Postmaster-General, is

responsible for its administration. The B.B.C. provides both education and entertainment to millions of people on payment of ten shillings to the State each year. Thirty years ago it would have seemed impossible that the State should supply the whole population, not only with educational talks, but with classical music, vaudeville, children's stories, cookery lessons, and jazz bands.

My second example you may see for yourself any summer Saturday afternoon if you ever go into Hyde Park and visit the Serpentine. I am old enough to remember what Hyde Park and the Serpentine were like on a Saturday afternoon in 1900, and I know that it would have seemed inconceivable then that the State should do what it does now to make ordinary people enjoy themselves there.

I will give you one more example of the way in which this democratic idea of happiness has changed things socially and politically in the last thirty years —the women's movement. During that time women have not only won the vote; they have established their right to enter professions, pursue occupations, and, if they want to, live the kind of life that men live. There can be no doubt that all this is due to the democratic idea that women have a right to every kind of happiness whether it comes from education or freedom and independence or work or amusements.

The main point of these examples is this: there

is no doubt, I think, that the ordinary lives of ordinary people are much happier to-day than they were thirty years ago and infinitely more happy than they were eighty years ago. Also nearly everyone now believes that it is a good thing to be happy, not once or twice a week on special occasions, but all the time if possible. That is really democracy and something comparatively new in the world. Even when I was a boy, people still believed that unless you were very rich or very well born, it was not right for you to be happy all the time. They still thought it wrong to be happy on Sunday, and indeed they made it almost impossible to be happy between midnight on Saturday and Monday morning anywhere in England. They still thought it wrong for a woman to find her happiness in medical or scientific work or for a domestic servant to find hers in playing the piano. They still felt it to be quite right in a civilized country that vast numbers of people, after working for ten or more hours a day, should have nowhere to spend their evenings except in overcrowded, badly built and badly lighted houses or in overcrowded but well-lit public-houses.

Democracy has taught us all that we have the right to be happy. It has, I think, made us on the whole a good deal happier. But merely by doing this democracy has also set us and itself a difficult problem. Nearly all great thinkers have said—and most ordinary people believe—that leisure is a very important thing, particularly in relation to happiness. A man who spent his whole life only in doing long hours of heavy manual labour and in eating and sleeping might not be unhappy, but his happiness would be of a rather narrow kind. It is from the employment of one's leisure time that perhaps the greatest happiness is possible. And it is here that democracy has made the greatest of all changes in recent years. It has not only for the first time in the history of the world given ordinary people who are not aristocrats or very rich a good deal of leisure time, time in which they can do what they like, but it has also given them various opportunities of employing their leisure time. The great difference between to-day and thirty or fifty years ago is that fifty years ago the State and society did practically nothing to provide the mass of the people with opportunities for employing their leisure, while to-day, in the B.B.C., in public libraries, adult education, parks, and playing grounds, such opportunities are provided.

But the way in which people use their leisure is of tremendous importance. Indeed, the difference between a civilized and an uncivilized person consists largely in the different ways in which they spend their free hours. Is it not your experience that the man who spends his spare time getting drunk and fighting is a very different kind of person from the man who spends his in reading and cultivating his garden? And I suggest to you that one of the chief problems before democracy is to provide people with means to employ their leisure well and to teach us to use them.

What are the forces which are acting against this democratic view of happiness? People who are Nationalists, Imperialists, Communists, or Fascists all hold political beliefs which are really inconsistent with the democratic view of happiness, and during the last thirty years the progress of democracy has been seriously impeded by Nationalism, Imperialism, Communism, and Fascism. The future of democracy is still threatened by them. I do not mean to say by this that there can be no good in Nationalism, Imperialism, Communism, or Fascism; all I mean is that one must face the truth that you cannot have them if you want to have democracy.

Look at it in this way. In a democracy the first thing which would be considered in all political questions would be how the everyday happiness of ordinary people would be affected. Now the nationalist or imperialist never really looks at political questions in that way. To him the nation or the empire is always much more important than the happiness of individuals. He regards all kinds of things, like glory, prestige, and power, as of more importance than the happiness of the ordinary citizen. The French nationalist to-day thinks it far more important that Alsace and Lorraine should not be separated from France than that the French social services should be improved. And the German nationalist before the war had the same kind of attitude. The British imperialist considers it much more important that India should be retained in the Empire than that the school-leaving age should be raised. That is why wherever there is Nationalism or Imperialism you find that the upkeep of a large army or large navy or both comes before the provision of social services or education. I am not now saying that the nationalist or imperialist may not be right; I am only saying that his views make it impossible for him to be a true believer in democracy, and that if people believe in Nationalism and Imperialism they cannot expect to get the happiness of democracy. The actual lives of hundreds of thousands of little French boys will be affected by the kind of education given to them in State schools during the next ten years; whether Alsace during that time belongs to France or Germany will probably affect the life of not a single one of them.

The nationalist and the imperialist are not the only people in the world to-day who are opposed to the democratic view that the main concern of government should be the people's happiness. Communists and Fascists do not agree in many things, but they agree in their dislike of democracy, and it is not surprising to find that both set up something different from happiness as the object of government. The Communist is a fanatic; he thinks that the Government should sacrifice everything, including if necessary the happiness of the population, to Communism. He might possibly say that, if Communism were once established, the population would be happy, but in practice that is not of much importance. In practice, as one may see in Russia, Communism is really a religion, and a Communist Government is prepared to sacrifice the happiness of vast numbers of people in order to establish Communism. The Fascists and the Fascist Government are exactly the same, only their religion is Fascism, and they are prepared to sacrifice the happiness of people in order to establish Fascism. Communists and Fascists also agree in two other points: they both act on the principle that the Government need not consider the happiness of those people who happen to be opposed to Communism or Fascism. They also both act on the principle that it is more important that a Government should be efficient than that it should make its subjects happy. In all these ways, therefore, Communism and Fascism are opposed to democracy.

Communism and Fascism are ideals, and there may be good things in these ideals. But in all the ways that I have mentioned their ideals are opposed to those of democracy, and that is why there is this struggle going on in Europe between the forces of democracy and those of Communism and Fascism.

3. EQUALITY

Do you believe in democracy? Then, if you do, you must believe in equality. For all democrats, in some sense or another, believe in equality, and this belief has caused immense political changes in recent years, as immense as the changes caused by the democratic idea about happiness.

The early democrats at the time of the French Revolution shouted for liberty, fraternity, and equality, and democracy is often represented as being little more than a belief that all men are equal. This democratic idea of equality may seem at first sight quite simple, as simple as the democratic idea of happiness, but it is not really very easy to understand and more nonsense has been written and talked about it than about most political subjects. I must therefore say a word or two about the meaning of democratic equality before I can explain some of the changes which have taken place in society during the last thirty years.

The democrat does not say that all men are or ought to be equal in every possible way. He says that for certain political and social purposes everyone ought to be treated as equal. For purposes of government and the organization of society, he says, people ought not to be treated as members of particular classes but simply as individuals. If you treat people as members of classes, you must treat

them as unequal; if you treat them as individuals,
you treat them as all equal. For instance, if you
have a law which says that only people paying rent
of more than £30 a year shall have the vote, you
are really dividing the population into two classes:
those with a certain income and those without it,
and treating them for political purposes as unequal.
But if your law says that every individual shall have
the vote, you are immediately treating everyone
for political purposes as equal. Again, suppose there
is a country in which women are not admitted to
universities and not given university degrees, are
not allowed to attend hospitals as students, and are
not given doctors degrees, in that country for certain
purposes connected with the medical profession the
whole population is divided into two classes, men
and women, the one able to become doctors and the
other unable—and you get social inequality. But if
you have a country in which every individual above
a certain age can study at universities, attend
hospitals, and take degrees, you immediately get
social equality so far as the medical profession is
concerned.

The point to observe is that wherever Government or Society treats everyone as an individual
and not as the member of some class, you get democracy and equality; wherever Government or
Society treats people not as individuals but as
members of some class, you get inequality and a
system which is hostile to democracy. Now there is

no doubt at all that many of the greatest political and social changes in recent years have been due to the growth of this democratic idea that people should not be treated as members of classes with particular rights and privileges, but that everyone should be treated simply as an individual of equal political value. Let me give you a few examples.

The most obvious example is, of course, to be found in the political and social machinery of the country, which has been almost revolutionized since 1900. Universal suffrage, votes for women, and the opening to them of universities, the professions and various trades and occupations all belong to the period since 1900, and they are all, in part or in whole, the result of this democratic idea that there should not be classes with special political and social rights and privileges, but that every individual should have politically equal rights and socially equal opportunities. This movement to abolish privilege of classes has, however, gone far beyond the mere machinery of government. Take, for instance, the rise of the Labour Party during the last twenty-five years. Twenty-five years ago the actual government of the country was still mainly in the hands of a narrowly restricted class or classes of aristocratically born and wealthy men. Professor Laski has shown that of the 69 Cabinet Ministers who held office between 1885 and 1905, 40 were the sons of the nobility, 52 were educated at Oxford and Cambridge, and 46 had been educated at public schools; and even between 1906 and 1916, 25 out of 51 Cabinet Ministers, i.e., practically half, were sons of the nobility. You have only to compare this with the personnel of the late Labour Government to see what a change there has been in this particular side of our social system.

Another extremely important direction in which democracy has done something to make people socially equal is education. Since a child's future happiness will depend a good deal upon his education, it follows, according to democracy, that the State should be very much concerned with education. But democracy also has something to say about equality; it says that the Government or State ought to treat everyone as an individual and not as a member of a class, and that it ought to see that, so far as possible, everyone is treated politically and socially as of equal value and given an equal chance of happiness. Now there can be no equality of opportunity, no equal chance of happiness, in a country in which one little boy, because he is born in one class, receives his education at one kind of school until he is twelve or fourteen years old, and another little boy, because he is born in another class, receives his education at another kind of school until he is eighteen or nineteen years old and then goes on to receive perhaps another three or five years' education at a university. It is therefore obviously impossible to have really and completely democratic society unless every child, no matter

what his father or mother may be or what their
income is, has the same educational opportunities.
This does not mean, of course, that everyone must
have exactly the same kind of education. All the
boys of wealthy parents do not have the same
education; if one is going to be a doctor, he has
one kind, and if another is going to be a barrister,
he is given another kind of education. But they all
have the same opportunities of choosing to be
educated as a doctor or a barrister, if they can show
themselves proficient enough. All the democrat says
is that all children in all classes should be given these
equal opportunities.

We saw in my second talk that a good deal has
been done in the last thirty years to increase the
educational opportunities of the less wealthy classes.
The State to-day provides much more and, on the
whole, much better education than it did in 1900.
Something has been done, too, to make it possible
for a certain number of children in those classes to
go on from the school to some university. But no one
can pretend that the educational system of our
country is to-day really democratic. Mr. Tawney's
recent book *Equality* shows quite clearly by statistics
—what I think most of us would have guessed—
namely, that unless you are the child of middle-
class parents who send you to a public school, your
chances in life are distinctly limited. For instance,
do you yourselves know any child, born of working-
class parents, who has become a Bishop or a Dean,

a Judge or a Police Magistrate, a higher Civil
Servant, the Governor of a Dominion, or the
Director of one of the big banks or great railway
companies?

Here, I suggest, is one of the great problems for
democracy and for the future. Whether democracy
is going to survive or not must depend to a very
great extent upon whether or not democracy is
really applied to education. Democracy will never
survive unless it is an educated democracy. Merely
by treating everyone as politically equal, by giving
everyone the vote, we are acting as if we intended
that everyone should be sufficiently educated to
understand the larger political questions and use
his vote intelligently. You cannot have such an
educated democracy unless the regular educational
system of the country is democratized.

It may be, of course, that this ideal is impossible.
If we have great wars and great armies and great
navies, the country may spend so much on these
things that it is impossible to afford the money for
education which would allow, let us say, the school
age to be raised to sixteen. Or it may be true, as
some argue, that the profits of our industries and
trade would shrink still further if our educational
system were improved and the children of other
classes were kept as long at school as those of the
middle classes. These ideas may be true, but one
ought to be quite clear in one's own mind what one
means if one accepts them. It means abandoning

the democratic ideal for some other ideal. If people want things which make great wars and large armies and navies necessary or great profits for trade and industry, they may not be able also to have democracy. But then they are themselves choosing things which make democracy impossible. Democracy in that case will not survive. But that does not mean that democracy might not survive if we were content not to have the great profits, the great armies and navies, and the great wars.

If you give a little time to considering the effects of democracy in the modern world, it is worth noting how widespread they have been in comparatively small things. For instance, when I was a boy, and even, I think, as late as 1900, the first class passenger on the railway was given a very comfortable seat; the second class passenger was given a fairly comfortable seat; the third class passenger was given a kind of wooden cattle truck with an intolerably uncomfortable seat. To-day the second class passenger has practically disappeared; he has been squeezed out of existence by democracy. And the third class carriage is very nearly as comfortable as the first. That is undoubtedly the result of the democratic idea of equality being applied to railway travelling, and the same kind of thing has happened in other small things that affect our everyday life.

What are the difficulties in the way of social equality? The greatest of all difficulties, perhaps,

has arisen in what is called the field of economics.
The democratic ideal of equality has in no country
of the world been applied to the distribution of wealth
and to property, though it is true that here and elsewhere something has been done in recent years to
make the distribution of wealth rather more equal.
The difference between the income of the very rich
and the very poor is probably to-day greater than
it was fifty or one hundred years ago, but in between
the very rich and the very poor there has been a
certain amount of levelling up and levelling down
of income, so that one may say that the standard of
living of large numbers of the middle class is less
different from that of Labour than it was even in
1900.

Now the early democrats and many people who
believe in democracy to-day believe that it is quite
possible to establish political equality or even social
equality and yet retain economic inequality. It is
most important to understand exactly what this
means. They believe that if everyone is given equal
political power by means of adult suffrage and equal
social opportunities by means of universal education
and in other ways, and if the rich are taxed much
more heavily than the poor, then you can establish
democracy and equality and at the same time leave
industry and trade, as it is at present, in private
hands and allow incomes to vary from a million in
the case of one man to £78 a year in the case of
another. But very early in the nineteenth century

other people began to argue that this was impossible. You will never get social equality or equality of opportunity, they said, unless you also have an equal distribution of wealth. It is absurd to pretend, they said, that the son of an agricultural labourer earning 25s. or 30s. a week, even though he goes to an elementary school and gets the vote at the age of twenty-one, will have the same opportunities in life as the son of a man with £500, £5,000, or £50,000 a year.

You will see that in these two views there is a tremendous difference of opinion, and the struggle between them has caused and is still causing great political and social changes in every country of Europe. On one side you have people attempting to work a system of political democracy and political equality with elected Parliaments and universal suffrage and to allow property to remain in private hands and finance, industry, and commerce to remain in private hands. To put it shortly, they are trying to combine democracy with what is called the capitalist system.

But the capitalist system in the modern world cannot work apparently unless a comparatively small number of people make very large profits, and everywhere it has led to great inequality in the distribution of wealth and national income. This inequality in the distribution of wealth and income clearly makes it difficult to establish any system of democratic equality. Liberals, who were in favour of democracy and equality and admitted the difficulty, have tried to remedy the inequality in wealth and income to some extent by heavy taxation of the rich—the supertax, for instance, and death duties, and to use the proceeds of these taxes for education, housing, and social services. But large numbers of people in the last fifty years have come to the conclusion that this is not enough. They believe that people cannot possibly have equal opportunities in life so long as the great inequalities in wealth which are inevitable under the capitalist system remain. They maintain that political democracy is a sham unless there is an equal distribution of wealth among all classes. It is this view which has led to the rise of Socialism, for the Socialist argues that democracy is not enough, that it is only by getting rid of the capitalist system and by putting the control of finance, industry, and commerce in the hands of the State or of the whole community that you will get a genuine system of social equality.

Consider Communism in relation to democracy. One may almost say that Communism, as understood in Russia to-day, is capitalism turned upside down. The Socialist wants to give to everyone an equal share of wealth and so equal opportunities in life. But the Communist goes to the opposite extreme. He definitely proposes to give a greater share of wealth to the manual worker than to other classes, and in so far he is opposed to the democratic ideal of equality. It is true that most Communists would probably say that this was to be only temporary and that they hoped eventually to establish a system of complete social equality. But in the world of to-day as we actually know it, Communism and Communists are opposed to equality.

Fascism and Facists are even more opposed to it. The democrat's ideal is a country in which everyone works together peacefully as equals and the Government does not bother about glory or power or prestige and treats everyone simply as an individual. The Fascist's ideal is a powerful, efficient, glorious State under the dictatorship of one man or one party. A dictatorship is necessarily based upon force, and in a Fascist State all force is concentrated in the hands of a class—the Fascist Party. The dictator treats you not as an individual but as the member of some class. If you are a journalist, he may give you one order, and if you are a railway porter, he may give you another. If you are a member of the Fascist Party your rights are quite different from those of a man who is not a member of the Party. Thus the Fascist rejects the democratic idea of equality just as we saw that he rejects the democratic idea of happiness.

We must all make up our minds upon this political and social problem which is disturbing the world. We may call ourselves democrats, but do we really believe in democracy and want it established in our own country and in our own lifetime? Are we prepared to see the abolition of all distinctions and privileges based upon class and to welcome complete equality of opportunity in education and choice of occupation, in material circumstances and political power? If we are, then we must also be prepared to make the sacrifice which a democratic system of equality would undoubtedly require from many classes. If we are not, then we must face the fact that we are joining those forces which are fighting against democracy.

4. LIBERTY

WE nearly all think that we ought to be able to do what we want to do. But do you also believe that other people ought to be allowed to do what they want to do? That is the terrific political question which was raised by democracy and has caused some of the greatest commotions and changes in the last 150 years. People often talk of democracy as if it were a material thing, something which you could pick up and put in your pocket, or at any rate something like a telephone service or a broadcasting system which can be installed in a country in a few weeks or a few months if the people decide that they want it. But democracy is nothing like that. It is really a way of looking at things, a political and social ideal, the ideas that people have of the kind of government they want, the kind of country or society or civilization they want to live in.

Suppose you were asked what kind of political system you thought there ought to be in England and what kind of society and civilization you would like to see there, you could not possibly answer in a single sentence. Your answer would have to be rather long and complicated. So too with democracy. You cannot define democracy in a single sentence, because it, too, tries to answer this question, What kind of government, social life, and civilization do we want? Democracy is, therefore, as you see, rather a complicated thing, for it must consist of a number of different ideas about politics and society and the lives that ordinary people ought to live. If large numbers of people have those ideas and insist that an attempt shall be made to put them into practice, then you will get one kind of government, country, and civilization, but if they have other ideas which are opposed to those of democracy and put them into practice, then the life which people live and the government which they enjoy or suffer under will be different.

I have already discussed two of these larger ideas which seem to me to underlie democracy and to have caused important political and social changes in our country and, indeed, throughout the world. The first idea had to do with the everyday happiness of ordinary people and the second had to do with equality. I am now going to discuss the third great democratic idea or ideal—liberty or freedom.

Before doing so, however, I feel that I ought to say one word of warning. I am treating these three ideas of democracy separately, and, indeed, each idea is different, so that a man may take the democratic view on happiness and liberty, but not on equality and so on. But these three ideas are also very closely connected. If a man wants one kind of life and political system, which for short we call democracy, he will find very soon that it cannot be established unless all three ideas of democracy about happiness, equality, and liberty are applied. And

that is why you will also find that people, like
Imperialists, Communists, and Fascists, who want
a different kind of life and government, are opposed
to democracy on all three ideas, happiness, equality,
and freedom.

The democratic idea of liberty is an easy one to
state and understand, but it has proved so far extraordinarily difficult to put it into practice. The
democrat believes that, so far as possible, everyone
should be allowed to do what he wants to do. That
means from one point of view that the Government
and Society should interfere as little as possible
with the individual, and from another point of view
that everyone should respect the right of others to
do what they like and should, therefore, live on the
principle of doing unto others as he would have them
do unto him. The democrat, you will observe, is not
a believer in authority and what is called discipline;
he thinks that people will be happier, more intelligent, more alive, and more civilized in a society
where everyone has an equal share in deciding
what should be done and where everyone is left
free, as far as possible, by the Government or State
to work out his own salvation, than in a society in
which a small class rules and the majority obeys, or
in which the State or the Government is continually
dictating to the individual what he ought or ought
not to do, say, and believe. On the other hand, the
democrat does not hold that there should be no
authority or interference by the Government with

individual freedom. People who hold that view are not democrats but anarchists. The democratic attitude may be defined as this: there should be as little interference as possible by Government and Society with individual freedom; but it is often necessary to compromise, to curtail the individual's liberty in the interests of other individuals and of the whole of society. But wherever such a compromise is necessary, our bias should be in favour of liberty and the benefit of any doubt given to the individual.

You will have seen how easy it is to state the democratic ideal of liberty, but what difficulties there must be in putting it into practice! Unless you are an out-and-out anarchist, you must agree to this continual compromise between authority and liberty. And once you have admitted the compromise, it is so easy to slip into the habit of paying lip service to democracy and at the same time of believing that everyone ought to be compelled to do what you think they ought to do and forbidden to do what you think they ought not to do.

We shall find, therefore, that it is with questions of liberty that the struggle between democracy and forces hostile to democracy has been most violent in recent years. Since 1900 in many respects the lives of ordinary persons have been greatly influenced by the growth of this democratic idea that it is good that everyone should, so far as possible, be allowed to do what they want. I will give you a few examples.

You must have observed in your own experience that large numbers of women and children now do what they want to do. But I assure you that the idea that women should be allowed to do what they want to do is extremely modern. Right up to the end of the nineteenth century most people believed—often unconsciously—that women should do what men wanted them to do, and social customs and even the law enforced this belief. The emancipation of women has really taken place in the last generation; no one can foresee its ultimate effects and it may prove to be one of the greatest social revolutions in human history. It is the direct result of democracy. But almost as remarkable as this revolt of women against the authority of men has been the revolt of the young against the authority of the old. In the nineteenth century it was still almost universally believed that in order to bring up a child properly, authority and discipline were the chief things necessary. Education, even as I remember it, consisted largely in teaching children to do what they did not want to do. One came half unconsciously to believe even that anything that one really wanted to do must be wrong. At boarding-schools the whole day was mapped out so that one was always acting under authority, always doing either compulsory work or compulsory games, and practically never left to oneself to choose what one wanted to do. At some public schools this curious system of education still exists, but elsewhere there has been a real revolution in education and the methods of bringing up children. Large numbers of people now hold that the object of education should be to help children to learn to do well what they enjoy doing. The result has been a great relaxation of authority and a great increase in the liberty of children and young persons. Old-fashioned, elderly people from time to time write letters to the newspapers deploring this fact. But it is the natural result of democracy applied to childhood and youth.

There are many other examples of this spread of individual liberty throughout society in recent years. There has been a revolt of the old as well as a revolt of the young. In the old days it was thought to be wrong, unseemly, or undignified for people to do quite a number of things after a certain age. No respectable elderly gentleman could go out in London without a top hat on his head and a pair of gloves on his hands; no respectable elderly lady could ride a bicycle or go on the top of a bus. To-day parents and grandparents, uncles and aunts, however elderly, are not subject to any discipline; they are allowed to do what they want to do without being thought eccentric or undignified. Again, the mere fact that there has been a growth of equality between the different classes also means that there has been an increase in individual liberty. The nineteenth century working man could not possibly do quite a number of things which to-day he would certainly be able to do, and it is not so very long ago, as the pages of *Punch* reveal, that it was thought ridiculous, if not immoral, for a domestic servant to want to play the piano.

There are other directions in which there has been an undoubted increase of liberty during the last thirty years. We still have some laws in this country which are certainly undemocratic, because they prevent people from saying or writing what they think on certain questions. But it is true, on the whole, that people are allowed to think, say, and write what they want to in a way in which they could not have done even twenty-five or thirty years ago. In other words, there has been a growth in the freedom of speech, the freedom of the Press and of the stage.

But what of the forces and ideas which are opposed to liberty? The democrat has to admit that a certain amount of authority and interference with individual liberty is necessary. The State or the Government, it is generally agreed, must in some ways prevent everyone doing exactly as he or she wants to do and must make everyone do some things for the general good. It is, of course, true that a certain amount of authority and regulation, though it may interfere with the liberty of some individuals, will actually increase the amount of liberty in the country. If the police make everyone drive on the left-hand side of the road, motorists find that they have much more freedom for driving cars than if everyone was left free to drive as he pleased. If all parents are compelled by the State to send their children to school until they are a certain age, the children will have much more liberty of choosing their occupations in after life than if the children of one class are educated for sixteen years and those of another for only six. It is for these reasons that side by side with the increase of liberty during recent years there has grown up an enormous amount of regulation by the State and of interference by the State with individual liberty. The State or the Government regulates your birth, health, education, insurance, old age pensions, and burial. It regulates the number of hours you may work, when and where you may drink alcohol or buy chocolate or cigarettes, when shops are to open and close, and any number of other things. In various countries it runs the post office, telegraph, telephone, broadcasting, tramways, railways, banks, shipping, and all kinds of other businesses and industries. This kind of system is, of course, called Socialism, and the Socialist believes that, in the interests of everyone, the State or the whole community should carry on industry and regulate some of our activities rather than leave them to the competition of private individuals.

The point to notice here is that the ideals of the democrat and the Socialist are not necessarily incompatible. The democrat can quite consistently say to the Socialist: "Of course, I agree with you that the good of the whole community is just as important as, indeed more important than the good of the individual, and I am willing to agree to State interference and regulation, but only on one condition, that you don't lose sight of the happiness and liberty of the individual. I can agree to State interference only if its result is to increase the happiness, equality, and liberty of all individuals." The democrat can say this to the Socialist, but in practice, of course, there is no doubt that the condition is not always fulfilled. Many people now believe that the State knows better what a person ought to do than he does himself, and quite a number of regulations and laws have been made on that assumption. The idea itself and the system which comes from it are undoubtedly hostile to democracy. Again, many Socialists and other people talk and think as if the State or the community were all-important and the individual of no importance. It seems to them positively good that the individual should sacrifice himself for the State or for the community, and they forget that after all the community is itself composed of individual men and women. Holding these views, they naturally propose and pass laws which leave little or no place for individual liberty and are therefore definitely hostile to the ideals of democracy. As examples of such anti-democratic legislation, I would suggest all censorship laws and regulations like the famous regulation making it illegal to sell chocolate in theatres.

There is no doubt that this problem of reconciling the claims of the whole community with the claims of the individual is one of the most difficult of all political problems—not only for democracy and democrats, but for all systems and for all people, no matter what their political beliefs. I would ask you to observe that there are forces at work in the world to-day that go much further than Socialism in demanding that the liberty of the individual should be sacrificed to the community. Both under Communism and Fascism the authority of the State over individuals is absolute. And Communists and Fascists seem to agree in thinking that there is something positively good in authority and discipline. It would not be unfair to say that they worship authority and that their ideal is a strong and efficient Government issuing its orders to an obedient and patriotic people. Here we have a point of view which is really fundamentally opposed to democracy, though it is in fact held by quite a number of people who are not Fascists or Communists. They do not believe that the great mass of people in any country should be allowed to do what they want to do or are capable of choosing their way of life or taking any part in political life. They point out the many difficulties which have arisen with parliamentary government and the weakness of many democratic Governments. Some of them maintain that the complicated system of industry, trade, and finance in European countries will not work if the wage-earners are given a share in political power which they can use for getting what they want in their economic life. Finally, they maintain that the ordinary man or woman is a much better person if subjected to authority and discipline, and that the population of democratic countries, where people are allowed to do what they want to do, becomes weak, cowardly, lazy, unpatriotic, and selfish.

There is a great struggle going on in the world to-day between the view which I have just described and democracy, and this struggle is causing some of the profoundest political changes.

But I want now to point out a curious element in our lives to-day which is quite different from Communism or Fascism, Imperialism or Nationalism, and yet seems to be working against the democratic idea of liberty, of everyone choosing his own mode of life for himself. Communism, Nationalism, and the other forces about which I have spoken are political systems which people are trying to put in the place of democracy. But the force which I am now going to refer to seems to be itself a result of democracy. I call it for short standardization.

In a modern democracy with universal education and a large number of State services there is a tendency for everyone to do, say, and think the same things, and instead of people choosing for themselves what they want to do and be, everything and everyone becomes standardized. Everyone tends to go to the same kind of school and to receive the same kind of education; we all wear the same kind of clothes; we all read the same kind of books;

the things we buy in shops are made by mass production in great factories and are all the same; newspapers with a million or two million or three million circulation give us all the same ready-made views on sweet peas one day and on politics the next. This standardization is well worth thinking about. It seems to me a kind of disease of democracy, for it destroys individuality and teaches people to follow one another like sheep instead of choosing for themselves. It is a real danger to the democratic ideal of liberty.

This question of standardization brings us to the root of the democratic ideal of freedom. Democracy has brought the world face to face with this question: Do you want to live in a society in which everyone is conscious of his individuality, thinks for himself, knows what he wants, and has the maximum amount of freedom, or do you want a society in which the majority are well-disciplined and obedient, and, like sheep, follow their leaders?

5. GODS OR BEES

THERE are two ways in which you can look at great political questions or at history. You can either examine them piecemeal, as if with a microscope, or you may take a bird's-eye view of them. I have been using the microscope so far. I have examined the various ideas about the happiness of ordinary people, about equality, and about liberty which have been working inside our own heads and operating in our country, our towns, and our villages, and which have caused those changes. I also showed that there are other ideas, forces, and movements in our industrial system and Communism and Fascism, for instance, opposed to these ideas of democracy and causing struggle and conflict in politics and society.

Now, if instead of looking at these ideas and changes piecemeal you put them together, as it were, and try to get a view of them as one whole, you will see, again, I think, that there is a great conflict going on in modern society between two different views about the sort of life that people should lead and the sort of civilization which they desire. Democracy is an extremely complicated ideal with regard to the lives which people ought to lead, the government they ought to have, and the civilization which they should aim at creating. The democrat has a vision of a society very different from any which is at present in existence. In it there would be complete social and political equality. Everyone would have equal opportunities and his place in society would be determined not by his class or birth or wealth, but by his abilities and his inclinations. It would be a society of educated and intelligent people in which independence of thought and speech and every kind of freedom and initiative were encouraged. In such a society the Government would be responsible to the whole democracy and its main function would not consist in issuing orders or disciplining the mass of the population, but providing for the everyday material happiness of the population, in trying to find out what people wanted to do, and in finding ways of making it possible for them to do it.

When the subject of these broadcast talks was first announced, one of the largest of the London daily papers had a paragraph in which the writer said: "I am amused to see that one series of talks, by Mr. Leonard Woolf and Lord Eustace Percy, is to be called 'Can Democracy Survive?' A series on 'Can Queen Anne Survive?' would be about as topical." The writer of that paragraph implied, of course, that democracy is dead. In that he was quite wrong and showed by his words that he had mis-read the history of the last thirty years. The great and numerous changes which I have discussed in previous talks—the changes in the machinery of our government, in the position of women, manual workers, and many other classes, in education and the social services, and in the way that all of us live, think, and amuse ourselves—all these changes show that democracy is still alive, for they are due to an attempt to create a kind of society and life which answers to the democratic ideal.

But the paragraph which I have just quoted also shows how strong are the forces opposed to democracy and how far we still must be from having a democratic system of government and a democratic type of civilization. These forces opposed to democracy are, like democracy itself, ideas, ideas inside the heads of people about the kind of life which they want to lead and the kind of civilization which they think desirable and attainable. I want now, if possible, to give a bird's-eye view of these anti-democratic ideals so that you may see the form of this great political and social struggle in which we are all living.

The democratic ideal, as I have described it, is a society of free, equal, active, and intelligent citizens, each man choosing his own way of life for himself and willing that others should choose theirs. The democrat is, you see, an optimist about human beings and human society; he wants us all to become like gods, free, independent people, forming our own views about the world and politics, and all co-operating in the State and in politics to build up a society in which men can live and think like gods. This ideal is an old one, and it was magnificently

stated over two thousand years ago by the Athenian
statesman Pericles when describing the Athenian
constitution in a speech to his fellow-citizens:

"We are called a democracy, because the city is
administered not for the few, but for the majority.
But although according to the laws everyone in
their private relations is upon an equality, yet
the man who is in any way distinguished receives
preference in public life, not as a privilege, but
because of his merits; and if a man can serve his
country, poverty or obscurity will not stand in his
way. Liberty is the principle of our public life, and
in our everyday life we are not suspicious or angry
with our neighbour because he pleases himself,
nor do we look upon him with the kind of dis-
approval which, though harmless, is annoying.
While we do not worry one another by interference
in private affairs, we are prevented from breaking
the laws by our respect for them; we obey both the
magistrates and the laws, and especially those laws
which are for the protection of the injured and
those unwritten laws which have the support of
public opinion."

That is the ideal of a democratic society. The
ideal which is most opposed to it and is causing
the greatest political conflict to-day can best be
described as the ideal of the beehive. The democratic
society is a society of individuals. In the beehive
you have in miniature a society of an exactly opposite
type. Every bee has his place and work in that

society allotted and defined for him. There are the
breeders, the nurses, the feeders, the workers, and
the fighters. No bee has any freedom of choice, no
initiative; he exists simply as a member of the hive;
he lives and works solely for the community or the
hive. Now, it would be quite possible for human
society to develop more or less along these lines of
the beehive, and the forces which are opposed to
democracy seem to me to be accepting this ideal
of the hive.

Think first of the industrial and capitalist system.
By that system I do not mean something in an
economic text-book or a Socialist's speech, but the
system of work and earning one's living in which
most of us spend the greater part of our days or
our lives. Consider those actual days and lives.
You may perhaps be an agricultural labourer. If so,
you probably left school for ever at the age of
fourteen and began to earn your living. There is
one whom I know myself. At half-past six every
morning he begins his work. I often hear him, for
he trudges past my bedroom window to fetch the
horses up from the meadows. His day's work ends
any time between 5 and 7.30 in the evening. He
works seven days a week, for someone has to look
after the horses on Sundays. I should like to say,
by the way, that he loves his horses and that some
time ago when there was a tremendous thunder-
storm in the middle of the night, I heard him go off
at two in the morning through a deluge of rain to

get them up from the fields. He is now old enough to draw an old age pension, but he still goes on working for a wage of 38s. a week. That is the life of an agricultural labourer. Or you may be a worker in a factory. In that case day after day for many hours a day you may go on doing the same operation all your life long in order to earn a few pounds a week. Or you may be a journalist; in which case you will perhaps sit in an office and correct proofs and write paragraphs all day or all night for six days a week in order to earn a salary of a few hundred pounds a year. Or you may be a business man or a successful barrister; in which case you will work ten or twelve hours a day in order perhaps to make an income of a few thousand pounds a year.

This is, of course, only a superficial account of the industrial and economic system in which we live. But so far as it goes, it is a true account and it shows you that in some way this system is very like that of the hive. It is much more like a beehive than like the society which the democrat hopes to create. The agricultural labourer, the factory worker, and the journalist, in their work at any rate, are much more like bees than like gods. Modern industry and finance are so complicated that businesses and factories and farms and the whole system have to be run like machines, if they are to be run efficiently, and the human being can no longer be treated as an individual, but merely as a cog in the machinery.

He is given his place in the system and he must go on hour after hour, day after day all his life performing the particular part allotted to him. But that is exactly the way in which the society of the beehive is worked.

Here, then, are the most powerful forces acting against the democratic ideal and making it difficult to establish a really democratic form of society. For how can the man who trudges past my window at half-past six in the morning and ends his day's work at half-past six in the evening, who left school at the age of twelve and is still working at the age of sixty-five for 38s. a week, how can he—good man though he may be and full of a kind of earthy wisdom—how can he have the knowledge, means, and leisure necessary if he is to play the part of a free, independent, equal, and intelligent member of a democrat State? Can you really say that he—or even the business man who works all day in his office—is independent and taking his part in the government of the country just because he has the right to vote at an election? Can you really say that he has any kind of social equality or equality of opportunity with the man who lives in a large house only three or four hundred yards from his cottage, a gentleman of independent means who was educated at Eton and Cambridge and now lives on an income of a few thousand a year?

The democrat cannot pretend that the lives which great numbers of people are forced to live under the present system are consistent with the democratic view of what civilization should be. Democracy has done something in the last thirty or fifty years to modify economic conditions by education, by social services, by taxation, and by reform of the franchise. But democracy has not yet succeeded in its struggle against these economic forces which are tending to make human society resemble that of the beehive. On the other hand, it was dissatisfaction with the industrial system and its effects upon the worker's lives which has caused the rise of Socialism. The Socialist proposes to alter the economic system by transferring its control from the hands of a small class of private persons to those of the whole community. As a rule, I think, he has usually been mainly influenced by the desire to ensure more equality of opportunity and a greater equality in the distribution of wealth. In so far as he does that he is really furthering one of the great ideals of democracy.

But Socialists have often, either consciously or unconsciously, also accepted the beehive as their ideal and model of what human society should be like. In order to get rid of the unfairness of the present system and give everyone the same chance in life, they are prepared to turn the State into an immense machine. Their view is that in this way everyone instead of struggling for his private profit, would merely do his work for the community and receive the same reward. But in fact that is just what happens in the beehive, and it is clear from Socialist experiments in Russia and elsewhere that Socialism, as at present understood, while aiming at equality forgets liberty and tends to produce the machine-like form of society in which the individual is merely a cog.

But there are other forces and movements that go much further than Socialism in accepting this ideal of the beehive. Many Socialists are or were also democrats and their desire, at any rate, is to combine the economic equality of Socialism with the liberty and independence of democracy. But in Communism and Fascism you can see two movements which have simply given up the ideal of democracy and are trying in the world of to-day to create a completely different form of society. The Fascist and Communist States are regarded as great machines, and like all machines we are asked to judge them by the efficiency with which they work. Thus the Communist asks us to admire the stupendous efforts to industrialize Russia and the success of the Five-Year Plan. If you discuss Fascism with a defender of Mussolini, he will very soon point with pride to the efficiency of the present Italian Government and to the fact that trains on the Italian State railways now start at and reach their destination at the right time. But they also have another ideal besides efficiency. Their view is that every individual should be regarded and regard himself simply as a servant of the community or the State. His duty is to serve the community. He must therefore gladly accept authority and discipline. His own opinions, independence, liberty are of no importance; what is of importance is only the Communist or the Fascist State, and for its sake he must take his orders and obey those in authority. Like the soldier, his not to reason why, his but to do and, if necessary, die.

If you look at Russia or go to Italy, you will see before your eyes an attempt being made to build up this new form of society. Or perhaps one should say that it is a very old type of society under a new name, for if you examine the pages of history you will find that before the eighteenth century society was always built upon authority and discipline rather than upon liberty and equality. At any rate, the Communist or Fascist in building his State is consciously rejecting the ideals of democracy. His ideal is service, authority, and discipline in order to obtain efficiency of government. Equality and independence of thought, speech, and act in ordinary people seem to him not good, but bad. His model is the hive, and the citizen of his State is to be a bee, not a god.

Communism and Fascism are, of course, extreme examples of this tendency in the modern world to abandon the ideas of democracy and to develop the machine-like society of the beehive. Even in our own country, in the England of to-day, you can see symptoms of it, both in the machinery of government and the political ideas which are inside the heads of ordinary people. The business of government has become so enormous and so complicated that the individual citizen feels that he has no control over or concern in it. Even the House of Commons and the Government find it more and more difficult to work this machinery. It is indeed largely controlled, not by the people nor by the Government, but by the Civil Service whose growth in numbers and power has been so remarkable in recent years. Thus both the economic and political structure of society tends to become more and more like that of a machine, and the individual, instead of feeling himself free and independent, feels that he is simply part of a great machine. But even that is not the greatest danger to democracy.

The greatest danger is that people tend to accept this situation and abandon the ideals of democracy for the ideals of mechanical efficiency. Both inside and outside the House of Commons you will often to-day hear people opposing measures which would make for democratic equality, liberty, and individual independence on the ground that they are inconsistent with industrial or governmental efficiency. To take that view is to regard society and government merely as a machine. The answer to those who hold it, and to the Communist and Fascist, seems to me to be this. Efficiency in industry and government is no doubt a good thing, but it is not the only thing. Even with a machine we do not judge it merely by its efficiency, but also by the things which it produces. For instance, personally I think the most inefficient machine for making chocolate creams is better than the most efficient machine for making poison gas, and I daresay most of you would agree with me. So too, with government, industry, and society. In the end they are to be judged not by the efficiency with which they work, but by the kind of lives and civilization which they produce for ordinary people. The lives lived by free, equal, independent people in a country where industry was not remarkably efficient and government did not go by clockwork might well be much happier and much better than those lived in the most efficient society where everyone did exactly what he was told to do by some dictator and lived the life of a bee.

But though what I have just said is, I think, true, I do not wish to ignore the difficulties of the political problem now facing the world. I will try to state it, as it shows itself to me, in the simplest form. How are we to reconcile the claims of the individual with the claims of the community in which he lives? Hitherto neither the democrat nor the Socialist has succeeded in doing this. The alternative proposed by Communists and Fascists and those who are dissatisfied with democracy and Socialism is to develop a society in which everyone is treated merely as part of a great machine. Can we possibly accept such a proposal? Is it not possible to combine the ideas of the democrat with those of the Socialist and so reconcile the claims of the individual with those of the community?

6. CITIZENS OF THE WORLD

I WONDER whether you have ever considered what political events have had most influence upon your own life and personal fortune. If you have ever done so, you will have made a curious and unexpected discovery. For undoubtedly the actual lives of the vast majority of us who have lived through the last thirty years have been much more profoundly influenced by what are called foreign politics or international relations than by any political event within our own country. The war which ended the lives of so many of our friends and relations and which has dominated the lives of those who survived it sprang directly, not out of domestic, but foreign politics. And the fall in the value of the pound which caused the crisis of September 1931 was an international, not a domestic event.

That seems to me, as I said, a curious and unexpected discovery. For suppose someone had said to you: "Which is more important to you?—to be an inhabitant of Great Britain or an inhabitant of the world?" I daresay you would have answered: "It is much more important to me that I am a British subject." But is that really true? To-day we are all citizens of the world as well as of Britain. Transport, trade, and the complicated way in which we modern people live have brought all countries so close together in so many different ways that we cannot isolate ourselves politically or economically. And so the murder of a Serbian prince, the difficulties of a bank in Amsterdam, or the boycott of cotton goods in Bombay may have a greater effect upon our lives than anything which happens in Westminster or Manchester. This fact points to one of the greatest of all the political changes of recent years. For what I have just said would not have been true during the nineteenth century. Had you lived and died before 1900, you would probably have spent the whole of your life without becoming aware that you were a citizen of the world or even an inhabitant of Europe.

The best way of seeing how democracy has affected and been affected by international relations in recent years is to consider actual examples. I have already very briefly referred to nationalism and imperialism as two forces in the world of to-day which are hostile to democracy and democratic ideals. Take nationalism first. When we speak of history or politics we are all consciously or unconsciously looking at these questions from the point of view of Englishmen or Britons. We never really forget that we are citizens of Great Britain or the British Empire. This sense of nationality is to-day one of the most powerful political forces in the world. But it has not always been so. It was only in the nineteenth century that large numbers of Europeans began to think that nationality was of the greatest importance politically and that all

Germans should be united together in one State, all Frenchmen in another, all Britons in another, and so on. At first nationality was not opposed to democracy, in fact it grew itself out of democratic ideas, and some of the great early nationalists, like Mazzini, were also great democrats. The ideal of democracy is a community or society of free and equal citizens and a State or Government whose principal concern is the everyday happiness of ordinary people. Now the nationalists, like Mazzini, applied this ideal from the relations between individuals and classes inside a single State to the relations between whole peoples of different nationalities. At that time, for instance, there was no Italian State, no Italian nationality. Large parts of Italy belonged to and were ruled autocratically by Austria. Italians, said Mazzini, have the same right to freedom and equality as Austrians, and all Italians should be joined together in a great free, equal, democratic Italian State.

Mazzini succeeded, and the same wave of national feeling swept over Europe and is still sweeping over it, creating here an Italian, there a German, here a Polish, and there an Irish Free State. If national feelings had stopped there, we could have said that the whole movement was not hostile, but favourable to democracy. But national feelings have become so violent in the last thirty or fifty years that what began as a movement for equality, freedom, and happiness has often turned into one of the most terrible political forces often making for oppression, violence, and war.

There are several reasons for this change. One is that the nationalist ideal is not really attainable. If you walk or drive from Land's End to Berwick-on-Tweed, you will find everywhere a people of one nationality, and it is quite easy for us to have a single national State in which within those boundaries we are all equal and of the same nationality. But all over Europe there are places in which that is not so. Suppose that all the inhabitants of Sussex were Germans, all the inhabitants of Kent were Czechs, and in Surrey half the inhabitants were Germans and half Czechs; that will give you a not unfair idea of how the population is distributed in many parts of Europe. But where the population consists of mixed nationalities in this way, you get what is called the problem of national minorities. Before the war there was a national minority of Poles in Russia, Germany, and Austria; to-day there are still national minorities in many States, of Germans, for instance, in Poland and Czecho-slovakia and of Austrians in Italy.

Now if these national minorities were content to be citizens of the States to which they belong, and if those States treated them according to the principles of democracy with regard to happiness, equality, and liberty, nationalism would not have to be counted among the forces hostile to democracy, and there would in fact be no problem of national minorities. But feelings of nationality are so violent that the majority of one nationality in these States nearly everywhere oppress the minority of the other nationality, refusing to give them equal political rights or the liberty to do what they want to do. The Polish State, for instance, seems to consider that the happiness of those of its subjects who are not Poles is of little account, and the same is true of the attitude of the Italian State towards its subjects who are of Austrian nationality. And partly because of this and partly because of their own violent national feelings, nearly all these national minorities live in a condition of permanent political discontent. They are always trying to separate from the State to which they are attached and to join a State in which the majority of the population has their own nationality.

You will see how inevitably nationality and nationalism are creating conditions in many parts of Europe which are extremely unfavourable to democracy. But the matter does not end even there. The process of cutting up Europe into national States has been going on with great speed and thoroughness during the last thirty years, and at the end of the war a whole lot of new States of this kind were created, Poland and Czechoslovakia and Jugoslavia, for instance. There is, of course, no reason why a man should not be very patriotic and also a democrat; indeed, I can never see why people should not feel great pride in the fact that they belong to a State in which all men and women are free and equal and happy. But if you look round the world to-day, can you see many or any countries where this is the case? Unfortunately it is a fact that in national States where feelings of nationality are strong, the democratic ideas about happiness, equality, and liberty are unpopular. The reason is that people there turn their patriotism into a kind of religion and their State into a kind of god. They insist that everything, including equality, liberty, and even happiness, should be sacrificed to the State and what they call nationality.

In this problem of nationalism the answer to the question "Can democracy survive?" seems almost to state itself. Democracy will survive only if people believe in it, if they want the kind of civilization in which States and Governments exist to protect the happiness, equality, and liberty of ordinary persons. But if they prefer the ideals of nationalism and national glory and a narrow patriotism, democracy must inevitably perish. And this is even more true of imperialism than nationalism.

Imperialism is a word used to describe that system by which immense areas of land and large masses of people in Asia and Africa have during the nineteenth and twentieth centuries been subjected to the rule of Europeans. Practically the whole of Africa and large parts of Asia have in this way been included in the Empires of Britain, France, and one or two other European States. Imperialism has, of course, often brought with it very real benefits in the way of law and order, health services, roads, railways, and so on, but here I am only concerned with the relation of imperialism to democracy. In this again we are really up against an international question, for it is a question not of the internal affairs of England, say, or Scotland, but of the political relations between the people of this country and the peoples of Asia or of Africa. The imperialist system seems to me to be the negation of democracy. It assumes that while Europeans are capable of deciding for themselves what kind of lives they want to lead and of managing their politics and their own countries in their own ways, inhabitants of Asia or Africa are incapable of doing so. The imperialist maintains, in fact if not in word, that Asiatics and Africans are by nature politically inferior to Englishmen and Frenchmen and Dutchmen, and that, therefore, it is only right and proper that the English, the French, or the Dutch should govern the countries inhabited by Asiatics and Africans, and should decide for these politically inferior people what laws they are to have and what lives they are to lead. Imperialism has, of course, been modified in many places in recent years under the influence of democratic ideas. For example, in India, Ceylon, and even some African possessions, the principle that the inhabitants should eventually govern themselves has been admitted. In so far as this change has taken place, imperialism has given way to democracy, and the British Empire may be gradually transformed in this way into a true Commonwealth of Nations.

I sometimes wonder whether, if an intelligent inhabitant appeared from some other planet and investigated the condition of Europe since 1914, he would not say at the end of his investigation: "Europe is inhabited by a race of extraordinarily stupid, incompetent, and arrogant people; though they have completely mismanaged their own affairs during the last seventeen years and nearly ruined all their own countries, they yet claim that they are the only people capable of managing the affairs of Asia and Africa." I am not at all sure that this might not be the opinion of an impartial observer of European history. The important thing to notice is that it is now the opinion of large numbers of the inhabitants of Asia and is becoming the opinion of a good many Africans. There has been no more important political change in the last thirty years than the political awakening of Asia. Everywhere the claim is being made that the democratic ideals of happiness, equality, and independence cannot be reserved as a perpetual monopoly of the white race. The Japanese, the Chinese, the Burmese, the Indians, the Persians, the Arabs, the Turks, and the Egyptians have all in turn revolted against Europe and denied the right of Europeans to dictate the kind of government they are to have and the kind of lives they are to lead.

Here is an international question closely connected with the survival of democracy. It is also one of those international questions which may have a great influence upon our own lives or those of our children. The future of the British Empire depends upon its solution. Democracy is an ideal which can be applied equally to the relations between individuals within a single country and to the relations between peoples inhabiting different countries. We can, if we like, aim at basing the British Empire upon authority and dictation. In that case the political status of the Asiatic or African will be inferior to that of the inhabitant of Great Britain or Canada or Australia. The Asiatic and the African will not be allowed to do what they want to do; the Englishman will decide for them the kind of happiness that is suitable for them; the sort of knowledge that is to be given or withheld from them; what occupations they are to pursue; what laws they are to live under. These peoples will be subordinated to Europeans on the plea that they are politically incapable of governing themselves, just as a little time ago in all European countries the common people were subordinated to aristocracies on the plea that they too were incapable of governing themselves. And if this system of domination, inequality, and inferiority is to be maintained, it will ultimately have to be maintained by force of arms.

On the other hand, there is no real reason why,

if we wish it, the principles of democracy should not gradually be applied to and extended over the whole Empire. It is merely a question of the kind of empire and the kind of civilization we desire. Democracy will survive in the Empire only if our object everywhere is that the Government should think first and last of the everyday happiness of the ordinary person and that the population should enjoy complete political and social equality and should be encouraged or taught to use liberty and independence—ideals which many people sincerely hold. That means that we must accept for the rest of the Empire those principles which we have already accepted in the case of the Self-Governing Dominions.

This problem of the British Empire is also the problem of the League of Nations, only there it is on a still larger scale. The ideals of democracy can be applied to the relations between ourselves and France or Germany just as they can applied to those between ourselves and India or East Africa. Before the war the relations between different countries were largely based upon a system of force and fraud, sometimes called diplomacy, and the war was its natural result. No British statesman in the nineteenth century would have acted on the assumption that in world government the happiness of the population of Germany or France was just as important as the happiness of the population of Great Britain. But if you really believe in democracy, you must in fact admit that that is the case, and in international questions you must act on it.

Now the League of Nations seems to me the very first beginnings of an attempt to apply these ideals and principles of democracy to world government. It is an attempt to create a system of world government in which the happiness of ordinary persons is the first consideration and liberty and equality are guaranteed. The League is perhaps a half-hearted and timid attempt in this direction, but it is at least the beginning of a new system in international affairs. It shows the immense importance of the fundamental ideas of democracy in the modern world. And its effect on our question "Can democracy survive?" is to substitute for it another question: "Can the modern world survive at all without democracy?"

LORD EUSTACE PERCY

7. NINETEENTH-CENTURY SOCIAL IDEALS

IN following Mr. Woolf I shall be covering a good deal of the same ground, but from rather a different point of view, and I would ask you to remember that it is only *my* point of view. I shall be discussing politics—that is to say, men's ways of managing their social life. The different ways in which men do manage their social life can only be understood by comparing different points of view. Of course there are certain facts about the social life of human beings which are not matters of opinion—psychological facts about how men usually behave in certain circumstances, historical facts about what men have thought and done in the past, biological facts about how heredity and environment affect our bodies and our minds. There are also certain moral principles about social life which are more than mere facts. For instance, we believe that slavery is wrong and freedom is right, quite apart from any facts of experience which go to show that slavery has certain undesirable results and that freedom is on the whole healthy. But when one has stated all these facts and principles, one finds that they hardly ever really account for the things that happen to nations. One always comes back to the biggest fact of all—the enormous part which is played in man's social life by mere good or bad judgment. Each of us can only bring his or her own judgment to bear on facts and principles. It is for each of you to compare your judgment with mine. I shall not be trying to convince you that my judgment is right; I shall only be trying to help each of you to form a judgment of your own. Our aim is understanding.

The first proposition I am going to put to you is, I think, a very good instance of the importance of judgment in considering political facts. In 1900 the peoples of the whole of Western Europe and America, and especially the people of Great Britain, had got what they had been striving after for the greater part of the nineteenth century, namely, commercial prosperity. The great political ideal of the nineteenth century had been the production of material wealth. That had been the avowed aim of statesmanship. In this, Great Britain had set the example during the first half of the century and other nations had followed her example in the second half. And it was this pursuit of wealth which led to the growth of British democracy.

We talk a great deal nowadays about democracy, but we seldom think what the word really means. Democracy means the exercise of political power by the mass of the people. But no one—at least no one who is worth his salt—seeks political power for its own sake. Men seek such power in order to attain some object. If that object is a worthy one, their power has a good chance of surviving; if it is unworthy their power will be temporary and insecure. That is how we judge the kings and dictators of history, and democracy—the power of the many—must be subject to the same judgment. The question whether democracy can survive depends upon the objects for which it is used.

What was the object for which the mass of our fellow-countrymen sought political power in the nineteenth century? I think they sought it mainly in order that they might have freedom to accumulate wealth. The 1832 Reform Bill, for instance, was the result of the revolt of manufacturers and traders in the new industrial cities against the domination of the landowners; later extensions of the franchise were due to the demand of the workers for a share in the power thus won by their employers.

Now, it is quite true that other political communities in earlier days devoted themselves to the production of wealth—the Italian cities during the Middle Ages, Flanders in the fifteenth and sixteenth centuries and Holland in the seventeenth century. It is quite true, too, that some of these earlier trading communities had been the pioneers of political and religious liberty. There is nothing necessarily materialistic about the effort to increase the wealth of the world. Nevertheless, if we bring our judgment to bear on a comparison between England in 1850 and Holland in 1650, I think we must admit that the Industrial Revolution and the preaching of the political economists from Adam Smith onwards had created a special political philosophy about the production of wealth which was different from anything that had existed in the world before.

It was different because the production of wealth became the only recognized standard of statesmanship. When Bentham, the great legal reformer, set himself to straighten out the tangle of English law as it had come down from the Middle Ages, he tried to clear away all the complicated legal maxims and fictions which had been invented to enlarge the powers of government and protect the privileges of this or that section of the population. He tried to substitute for all these a simple principle to which the law should conform: "the greatest good of the greatest number."

In much the same way the political economists set themselves the task of straightening out the equally tangled system of restrictions on trade and industry. They saw that "the greatest good of the greatest number" of mankind a hundred years ago —what the great mass of mankind most needed— was a greater quantity of the mere necessaries and ordinary comforts of life. They therefore translated Bentham's principle into something like this: "The greatest quantity of goods for the greatest number." But the greatest number could only get the greatest quantity of goods if the goods were cheap, and cheap production meant mass production, and mass production meant division of labour—a system under

which the working life of each individual is concentrated on making one particular part of something.
And so we get another principle: "the production
of the greatest amount of goods by the efficient
organization of the greatest number of people into
a co-operative labour force, each individual performing one particular job."

Now what has been the result of this? The result
has surely been that the interest of each individual
as a worker taking a pride in his work has been
subordinated to his interest as a consumer getting
a greater quantity of goods more cheaply at the
price of a working life of comparative drudgery.
The world is divided into two sorts of people: those
whose main interest in life is their work and those
whose main interest is their leisure. The philosophy
of the nineteenth century amounted to this: that
the mass of mankind should feel little interest in
their work, and should be compensated for the
dullness and pettiness of their work by getting an
increased amount of money to spend on their leisure,
and more leisure in which to spend it. "Economic
efficiency" became the great cardinal virtue. Cottage industries were "uneconomic" and so they had
to go. It was true that such industries helped to
make the family of the farmer or the agricultural
labourer self-supporting and independent, but people
like Cobbett, who argued this and inveighed against
the "lords of the loom" who were making it impossible for the farmer to dress himself in homespun

cloth, were derided as reactionaries. According to the new philosophy, it was not the business of human beings to be independent or self-supporting; it was their business to regard themselves as members of a great co-operative army engaged in a campaign for the accumulation of wealth, with the prospect of sharing increasingly in that wealth.

This political philosophy was not, of course, invented by the nineteenth-century radicals. It had started much earlier with the Whig and Tory landlords, especially in East Anglia and the Midlands, who undertook the improvement of agriculture at the cost of abolishing the old inefficient system of open-field cultivation. The enclosures were supported by the natural enemies of these same landlords—the "progressives" and radicals—in the sacred name of economic efficiency; and, in a sense, they were right.

The same philosophy was adopted by Marx and his Socialist disciples who, as it seems to me, differed from the radical political economists only in believing that the mass organization of labour should be carried out directly by the State. It is significant that the only practical experiment in Marxian Socialism on a large scale, the Russian experiment, is based on the complete denial of any claim by the individual workman to any kind of economic independence. The Soviets have really carried the political philosophy of the nineteenth century to its logical conclusion; communal economic efficiency is everything. Every school of political thought in the nineteenth century really adopted this idea of the accumulation of wealth as the sole end of society, and in 1900 no schoolboy, no university student, was allowed to doubt it. We were taught, and believed, that men like Cobbett and Ruskin, who had attacked this idea, had been proved wrong —that they were mere cranks who had for a short time yapped at the heels of the inevitable march of human progress.

But supposing that I am right in this view about the main aim of democracy in the nineteenth century, am I right in saying that in 1900 we had attained the commercial prosperity that we had been striving for? Is it possible to take such a view, in face of the poverty of the great mass of the population in all civilized countries? I think it is; or rather I think it is true to say that we had secured all the benefits that mankind can secure by mere commercial prosperity. Nor ought we to underrate those benefits. Taken as a whole, the wage-earners in Great Britain were nearly twice as well off in 1900 as in 1850, and recent researches seem to prove that the actual wealth of the wage-earners, expressed in spending power, had been increasing pretty steadily for a century before 1850. The evils we were suffering from in 1900, and had suffered from even more in the earlier years of the century, were really the direct result of this striving after commercial prosperity, not a sign that we had not yet attained such prosperity. Let us examine these evils for a moment. They were of two kinds.

In the first place, the continual mobilization of great masses of men for the purpose of large-scale production resulted in the concentration of human beings in large centres of population. Hence the problems of bad housing and overcrowding. The depopulation of the country districts got rid indeed of a vast number of houses quite as bad, and indeed much worse, than the workers' dwellings in the cities. In fact, so far as mere bricks and mortar are concerned, it would probably be true to say that housing steadily improved, but indifferent housing in the great cities creates much worse conditions than even the worst housing in country villages; and a crowded city life produces social evils of its own in a population unaccustomed to such life. The movements of population which followed the Industrial Revolution thus produced social evils, not because they reduced the material wealth of the workers, for they actually increased it, but because they changed the living conditions of the workers so quickly that the workers had no time to adapt themselves to the changes. It might almost be said that for many years the social condition of the workers deteriorated in proportion to the increase in the purchasing power of their wages. They probably ate more and better food, but in other respects their increased wealth remained ineffective. It was only gradually, in the later years of the century, that they found ways of spending their money in a better use of their leisure. Even up to the war, their standard of clothing remained remarkably low.

In the second place, in 1900 we were less well equipped than many other countries with what are generally called "social services," i.e. those services which can only be organized by communal action. We probably led the world in factory legislation and the restriction of child labour, in sanitation, in hospitals and in the isolation of infectious disease, but we were behind most other countries in education, and we were behind Germany in social insurance against old age and unemployment. But this again was largely due to our political philosophy about the accumulation of wealth. The capital of the country was fully employed in extending trade. True, some of that capital was employed in the production of luxuries, when it might have been better employed in the production of simpler comforts required by the mass of the population, but it was an essential feature of the whole scheme of mass production which we had adopted that capital should be continually accumulated for the purpose of extending and improving the machinery of production. Any expenditure which interfered with this was regarded as so much slowing down of the economic progress of society.

And here we come up against the really weak spot in this whole political philosophy. What I am going to say may not be completely accurate as a proposition in economic science, but I think it is sufficiently accurate for practical purposes. A particular society, Great Britain, for instance, can only continue indefinitely to increase its wealth by division of labour and mass production if its adult citizens continue indefinitely to produce and sell more of the goods on which their labour is employed than they themselves can consume. In other words, it can only continue to increase its wealth so long as its population continues to increase and so long as it can continue to sell more and more goods to other countries.

Our success in the nineteenth century was due to the fact that not only was our own population increasing rapidly, but we were manufacturing many things for the whole civilized world. We were, moreover, continually extending the frontiers of the civilized world by settling new countries on the American continent, by opening up the Far East to our trade and by teaching uncivilized people in Africa and elsewhere to buy our goods. When Mr. Stiggins in *Pickwick* raised money to send "moral pocket handkerchiefs" to the "little niggers" in the West Indies, he did what our whole nation was doing throughout the nineteenth century, and what alone enabled us to succeed in our aim of accumulating wealth rapidly.

But in 1900 there were already signs that this process could not continue indefinitely. The birth-rate was falling in this and other European countries, and the settling of new areas on the other side of the Atlantic was therefore slowing down. European countries, instead of giving us growing markets for our products, had themselves become great manufacturers and were competing with us in overseas markets. India and China, too, as well as Japan, had begun to compete with us. Moreover, we had opened up practically the whole world to our trade; there were no new worlds to conquer. If the political philosophy in which we had been brought up could only work by the continual opening up of new markets, it was already clear that it might cease to work altogether in the near future.

That is what makes 1900 a real dividing line in history. The world that went into the Spanish-American War and the Boer War was a world completely satisfied that it had solved the secret of political well-being and progress; the world that came out of those wars was a doubtful and rather anxious world, wondering whether after all the political philosophy of the Victorian era was the last word in human wisdom. And these doubts were justified. It seems fairly clear that the growth in the spending power of the mass of the population in this country, which had continued steadily up to 1900, as we have seen, was arrested between 1900 and 1914. During these first fourteen years of the century the real wages of the worker seem to have remained almost stationary. That, at any rate, was a belief widely held just before the war and was one of the main arguments used by the Labour Party in favour of a new distribution of the national wealth.

Hence the change in political outlook which undoubtedly took place between the last ten years of the nineteenth century and the first ten years of the twentieth century. Whatever may be the correct figures of the growth in national wealth over this period, there is no doubt that between 1890 and 1900 men looked at unemployment and financial crises and gold shortage and all the other economic problems of the time as temporary difficulties and set-backs in the march of economic progress, while between 1900 and 1910, although towards the end of that period general economic conditions were perhaps better all round than at any time during the twenty years, men had a growing feeling that all was not well and that the future was uncertain.

We did not, alas, change our political philosophy; we continued to use the production and accumulation of wealth as our sole political standard; Socialists who attacked our existing social system continued to attack it on the ground that the wealth produced was unfairly distributed, not on the ground that the social system was too exclusively devoted to the rapid accumulation of wealth. But our confidence in the success of our political philosophy was beginning to be undermined. These dawning doubts were the real reason why the turn of the century destroyed the old comfortable political division between Conservative and Liberal, produced a new Labour Party, and set the Conservatives and Liberal parties hunting after new policies—protection and imperial preference on the one hand and social insurance and the 1909 budget on the other.

It is necessary to remember how reasonable and humanitarian were the political ideals of the nineteenth century. The raising of the material standard of living of the mass of mankind as rapidly as possible is no unworthy ideal. On the contrary, it requires a rare kind of far-sightedness to see the flaws in it. It is quite possible, and I think probable, that our grandfathers were right in thinking that an increase in the earnings of the mass of the people was more effective in raising their standard of living than any number of communal social services. The only fault of these political ideals is that they are one-sided. Our question is "Can democracy survive?", but the question whether the democracies of the Western world will survive depends mainly, not an any abstract argument about democracy as a form of government, but on the question whether the political philosophy to which the Western democracies were wedded in the nineteenth century deserves to survive and whether these democracies can devise better objects for the exercise of their political power in the future.

8. POLITICAL CONSEQUENCES

As Mr. Leonard Woolf remarked, the things that happen in the political life of a nation are the result of the political ideas held by the citizens of that nation. The first result of the political ideas of the nineteenth century was the extension of the franchise by the Reform Acts of 1832, 1867 and 1885. I have already pointed out that the Act of 1832 was the direct result of the desire of the new manufacturing cities to sweep away the old restrictions on trade in order that they might have freedom to accumulate wealth more rapidly; the Acts of 1867 and 1885 were the result of the desire of the workers to share in the political power thus won by the manufacturers and traders. But it seems to me that there was not really a very strong popular demand behind these extensions of the franchise in 1867 and 1885. Moreover, it is important to remember that these three Acts only gave the vote to a comparatively small minority of the population, and yet during the first fourteen years of the present century there was very little demand for a further extension of the franchise, even taking into account the woman's suffrage movement. People, indeed, wanted "the vote" because they felt that, if their neighbours had it, they had a right to it too; but when all is said and done they did not want it very keenly, because they did not want to do anything particular with it. The manufacturer and trader wanted free trade; the workers wanted freedom to combine in trade unions for collective bargaining and factory laws to improve the conditions of their work; but once they had got these things, they wanted simply to be let alone to accumulate wealth by manufacture and trade, and to get the best distribution of that wealth by collective bargaining. They did not want much more from Parliament, at any rate until after 1900: up to that time, at least, democracy to the mass of our people in the towns meant trade unionism rather than parliamentary politics. It is quite true that many working men had a very high idealism about such things as education, but one must not forget that the Education Act of 1870 was very unpopular indeed at the time.

The next result of the political ideas of the nine-teenth century I have also touched on briefly: social services. The concentration of the population in great cities created health problems which could only be dealt with by communal action. Hence came the sanitary services, the hospitals, and the beginnings of town planning and housing reform. In all these, and in our factory and child labour laws, we led the world. But we did less for educa-tion and social insurance than other countries, because we believed it was more important, in Mr. Gladstone's words, to leave wealth to fructify in the pockets of the people than to tax them for communal services like education which were thought to have no direct connexion with the main business of producing and selling goods.

But the social services we did start produced a third result: a great extension of local government. It was here, in the borough councils, the rural and urban district councils, and finally the county councils, that, as it seems to me, our fathers began to establish real democracy. The people, the ordinary man and woman in the street, changed the face of the country in the last twenty-five years of the nineteenth century through the work of these local councils, while Parliament still remained more or less the same as it had been since the 1832 Reform Bill. A man in 1900 reading an old political novel, like Trollope's *Phineas Finn* or one of Disraeli's, could easily recognize in it the House of Commons he knew, in spite of all differences; but a man reading Kingsley's *Alton Locke* would find it difficult to recognize in it the London of the Metropolitan Board of Works and the London School Board.

There was a fourth result which was a most curious one: the British Empire. We did not want to govern an empire, but we did want markets with which we could trade freely. We were rather bored by our great colonies; our first instinct, even the instinct of Disraeli in his younger days, was to give them self-government and let them go. But as anarchy was bad for trade, wherever we found disorder in the world—in India or in China—we itched to put things right.

In any case, we were out to protect our own traders in uncivilized or semi-civilized countries: and we soon found that it was equally necessary to protect the natives of such countries from the least scrupulous of our traders. And as it gradually became clear that we were the only country that was going to adopt Free Trade, we came to feel that the only way to get new markets was to own them ourselves. At the same time other nations, also needing new markets, came to feel that they would rather see Great Britain in control of these markets than any other country, because a British market would at least always be open to their trade. And so there grew up in this country a queer kind of policy, half imperialism and half impatient abdication of irksome responsibilities in our over-seas dominions.

That policy created the British Empire—but it may almost be said to have created it by mistake. Perhaps the truest thing ever said about our government of India in the middle of the nineteenth century was said by Bagehot in criticizing John Lawrence's administration of the Punjab: "In seven years the Punjab was transformed from a native state, in which anarchy was universal and careers numberless, into a British province in which order was as settled as in Kent and nobody was allowed to do anything except make money." That was how we introduced our own nineteenth-century philosophy into the East.

That is a rough account of the results of our nineteenth-century ideas up to 1900. But at the turn of the century a great change took place—a change in our state of mind—a change from self-satisfaction to doubt and anxiety. And our anxiety changed our whole political policy.

It did not indeed, as I have said, create much demand for manhood suffrage; but it created a strong and compact Labour Party in the House of Commons with a distinctly Socialist policy. This was the outward and visible sign in Parliament of a great change of policy in the country.

First came an extraordinary revolution in education policy—the Education Act of 1902. Having been behind most other countries in education we began to take the lead. There followed John Burns's Housing and Town Planning Act, the creation of the Labour Exchanges and the group of Social Insurance Acts—Old Age Pensions, Health Insurance, and the first Unemployment Insurance Act. All this legislation resulted in an extension of the powers and responsibilities of the local councils. In particular, the new Education Committees created by the Act of 1902 added a vast field to the domain of local government.

The ideas behind this social reform movement were mixed. To a great extent we were still aiming at economic efficiency. Germany was regarded as the most economically efficient nation, and we were eager to bring our education up to her level and to copy her employment exchanges and her schemes of social insurance. But with all this and dominating all this was our growing anxiety at the slowing down of the economic progress of the mass of our population. The earnings of the workers were not apparently increasing in value: the unemployment which we experienced in the first ten years of the century seemed to be due to deeper causes than any temporary fluctuation of trade.

A new idea, therefore, which had begun to emerge before 1900 took possession of us: That of redistributing wealth, not by collective bargaining between workers and employers, but by taxation. This was a compromise between Socialism and the old individualism of the nineteenth century. The State was not to take over industry in order to raise the workers' wages, but was to add to the workers' wages by drawing off some of the profits of industry and returning them to the workers in the form of pensions, insurance benefits, free education, and so on.

And here we come up against one of the least expected and most important effects of our nineteenth-century political philosophy: the growth in the power of the State. Our grandfathers had thought that the less the State interfered with the production and distribution of commodities, the more rapidly would wealth accumulate. But at the same time they were always insisting on communal efficiency and they thought that the accumulation of wealth was the one great aim on which all the energies of the community should be concentrated. They felt no inconsistency therefore in encouraging their Government to open up China to foreign trade, even if it had to be done by the guns of battleships. It took a man of very independent mind, like Lord Salisbury, to refuse to put the machinery of Government in motion to support a British trader in an out-of-the-way corner of the world on the ground that "Buccaneers must expect to be uncomfortable." Our grandfathers did not see that, on their own principles, if the accumulation of wealth began to slow down, if communal efficiency failed to produce the results expected from it, and if no one could exactly explain what was wrong, the Government of the State, as representing the community, would be forced to take an active hand and to try to find a remedy by State action.

And this is what actually happened. It began to happen first on the continent of Europe. There, owing to force of circumstances, the nineteenth-century philosophy of the accumulation of wealth was combined with another and more inspiring philosophy—the idea of nationality. The middle years of the nineteenth century were occupied by the creation of two great new States, Germany and Italy, as well as a number of smaller ones such as the Balkan States. The whole idea of nationality as the basis of the political organization of the world only dates from the French Revolution.

The idea was that each group of people who spoke a common language and had a more or less common history of development had, as Mazzini said, "One line of God's message to mankind written on their cradle"; and the members of each such group must be able to control their own destinies through a common government of their own, in order to carry out their mission. Fichte, one of the great educational leaders of Germany one hundred and twenty years ago, had preached much the same doctrine in his *Addresses to the German Nation* in the dark days before the German War of Liberation against Napoleon in 1813. The German educational system drew its inspiration from that war of liberation. Each nation had a right to a "place in the sun" for its culture in order that it might carry out its peculiar mission.

But in the last twenty-five years or so of the nineteenth century, when these nations had achieved their unity and independence, they realized that they needed also a place in the sun for their trade. This was the place they had most obviously missed, for Great Britain had taken their place while they had been struggling for national liberty and unity. Consequently their new Governments began at once to take a direct part in stimulating industrial production and promoting economic efficiency. Hence Germany's social policy, to which I have already referred. This pursuit of economic prosperity practically obliterated the republican ideas which had supplied so much driving force to the nationalist movement ever since the French Revolution. To the horror of English Liberals like Mr. Gladstone, who had taken so much interest in the nationalist movement, democracy as a political ideal took a back seat in the new nations. But the new nations were only copying the old England. Economic efficiency had become everything.

And they copied England particularly in one practical way. Both Germany and France embarked, far more deliberately than England had ever done, on a Colonial policy. By 1900 both France and Germany had become great colonial Powers. Italy groped slowly in the same direction till at last her colonial ambitions flared out in her war with Turkey in 1911.

Just about 1900, too, Great Brtiain for the first time became, so to speak, conscious of her Empire. Disraeli's action in making the queen of England Empress of India was perhaps the first step in this direction; Cecil Rhodes's deliberate policy of creating a great British colonial empire in South and Central Africa, extending as far north as the Sudan, was perhaps the second; Joseph Chamberlain's choice of the Secretaryship of State for the Colonies as his office in Lord Salisbury's Government in 1895 was perhaps the third. Then the Empire seemed to focus itself in a flash in the South African War. The rather aimless Colonial Conferences became an Imperial Conference. From 1900 onwards men were continually asking themselves the question what the Empire was or ought to be, and the question how the Empire could be used to restore the lagging commercial prosperity of Great Britain was never far from their minds.

The United States meanwhile was following rather a different course. Her vast internal market and a constant stream of immigration postponed for her the problems which were creating anxiety and unrest in other countries, but she did begin after 1890 to feel a certain uneasiness which found expression in more drastic protective tariffs, a stricter control of immigration, anti-trust legislation, and a growing social reform movement.

To sum up. What was happening to the world in these years between 1900 and 1914? Three things mainly:

First, in every country Governments were taking a more and more active part in encouraging or protecting their trade. In Great Britain, where our industries and our trade seemed no longer to be securing a steady rise in the workers' standard of living, we were trying to raise that standard of living by State action and taxation. In doing so we were interfering more and more with the individual's freedom of choice and action. It is worth considering whether strict laws of compulsory school attendance and compulsory insurance conflict with the principle of democracy; but it is even more worth considering whether such measures, coming on the top of a century-old social movement restricting the individual's sense of freedom by concentrating the population in great cities, do not threaten to sap the spirit of reasonable independence which is the salt of human life. You have to look at the cumulative effect of all these things, not at one isolated piece of legislation. At any rate, in my opinion, it is a very dangerous state of mind in a democrat to identify democratic educational reform with the raising of the age of compulsory school attendance, as Mr. Woolf seems to do. It is also a grave question how far our attempts to redistribute wealth by taxation before the war were, or would have been, effective in raising the standard of living of the masses of our people. The war, however, introduced new factors into this question. There are, I think, only two results that we can be sure of: that our education in 1914 was out of all recognition better than in 1900 and was doing much to raise the general level of intelligence and character in our people; and that the local authorities were fairly launched on a policy of housing and slum clearance which promised steadily to improve their living conditions. I will suggest to you that these achievements were not connected with any restrictions on individual liberty. It was the growth of our higher education, not the stricter enforcement of compulsory attendance in the elementary school, which did so much for our people.

Secondly, the Governments of all the Great Powers,

except the United States, were building up or trying to build up colonial empires for the improvement of their trade. From these efforts arose continual friction in every part of the world. At the end of the nineteenth century there was such friction in the Far East; at the beginning of the twentieth century there was much more serious friction in North Africa.

Thirdly, more serious than any frictions about colonies, was the ever-present and ever-growing clash of competition between the industrialists and traders of different nations in every market of the world, and the ever-growing anxiety in every nation as to whether there was enough trade to go round —enough to keep the organization of mass production by division of labour going in all the countries which had committed themselves to that kind of organization as the sole basis of their prosperity. That anxiety was greatest in Great Britain, which had specialized most of all in the mass production of manufactured goods for export; it was perhaps least in France, which had always refused to sacrifice the ideal of a self-supporting peasant agriculture to the idol of economic efficiency.

Out of these three factors there came during these years a growing sense of deadlock, a feeling that the world had grown too small for the energies of mankind. In 1913 indeed the world seemed to be temporarily relieved of its anxieties by a period of prosperous trade. But the harm had already been done. The idea of democracy had become tied to the idea of a rapid accumulation and distribution of wealth, resulting in the crowding together of masses of men under conditions in which they could have no feeling of self-support or independence. Those crowds had, in the long run, to be organized; and they inevitably tended to be organized on a national basis. Crowds of people may jostle each other in a theatre queue without any dangerous result, but when they begin to organize themselves into groups for the purpose of concerted jostling it is time for the policeman to begin to take notice.

And if it is not a theatre queue but a bread queue, and the crowd begins to fear that the baker's stock is running short, the policeman had better think of telephoning to headquarters. A wise policeman will not stop to argue whether organized crowds are a good or a bad thing in themselves, nor will he make the mistake of supposing that the leaders of the organized groups in that crowd are moved by the ambition to kill the baker and take the shop for themselves. The first question we have to consider is not whether democracy in the abstract can or ought to survive, but whether the things that democracies do at any given moment are wise or foolish. The worst mistake is that which was made by some people at the outbreak of the war, of supposing that a state of nerves in the peoples of the world is to be attributed to the naughty ambitions of a few statesmen. The one thing of which we can be sure is that a policy, whether conducted by democracies or tyrants, which prevents men getting bread except by joining in a crowd, is a dangerous policy for the peace of the world.

9. THE CATASTROPHE

WE have come to the threshold of the war. I have not attempted to define the causes of the war, but I have tried to describe the anxious and oppressive atmosphere of deadlock which preceded the war—the universal sense of overcrowding and insecurity. Consider now some of the results of the war.

Broadly speaking, it seems to me that the war intensified all the tendencies, good and bad, which I have been trying to trace. In old days men used to regard all catastrophes as "judgments" on the world for its sins. We don't much like using theological language of that kind to-day; but as a matter of fact that language is perhaps more scientific than a good deal of our modern jargon. It is true that catastrophes like the war do tend to demonstrate and force men up against the logical conclusion of their beliefs and the natural consequences of their acts. In that sense they do constitute a "judgment" of those beliefs and acts.

To begin with, the war produced in this country, in a most spectacular way, precisely the redistribution of wealth after which we had been groping ineffectively before the war, and it produced it in precisely the way that our grandfathers hoped to produce it—by a general increase in the wages of the manual worker. The last ten years have been so full of troubles, in particular we have been so oppressed with the problem of unemployment, that we tend to forget the revolution in spending power and standards of living that was brought about by war wages. To take one concrete instance, it used to be said that the English manual worker was distinguished by the badness of his clothes; but to-day the manual worker is as well dressed in his leisure hours as the professional worker. Some of us pay more for our clothes than others, but, except at Ascot and such special occasions, we all dress alike. This, and not the spectacular profits made by a comparatively small number of people, was the outstanding result of war conditions in industry. And in this the war only intensified and demonstrated the main trend of economic development during the preceding century.

It is often said, and I notice that Mr. Woolf has said it, that capitalism has led to great inequalities of wealth. This is really historically inaccurate, as I have tried to indicate. Industrial capitalism results in a great accumulation and concentration of wealth, and these accumulations tend to be *controlled* by comparatively few people, some of whom, owing to their control, become extremely wealthy themselves, but the *ownership* of this wealth tends to be much more widely diffused under a system of industrial capitalism than in a society like eighteenth-century England where wealth is held mainly in the form of land. The war profiteer, like the pre-war Carnegies and Rockefellers, was only, so to speak, a highly coloured advertisement of a state of widespread financial prosperity.

At the same time the war produced another marked and far-reaching effect on the living conditions of the mass of our people by materially reducing their normal hours of labour and increasing their leisure.

But this prosperity was largely fictitious. The whole nineteenth-century philosophy of what Mr. Woolf calls the bee-hive depended for its success on the continual accumulation and reinvestment of the growing wealth of the community. But in the war we were not accumulating but were rapidly dissipating wealth, and both the war profits of the few and the war wages of the many were really so many promissory notes representing, not an increase in the present wealth of the community, but the hope that, after the war, industry would be able rapidly to restore the wealth which the war had destroyed. We are all conscious of the tremendous burden of our national debt which represents only wasted wealth and which nevertheless must be repaid, but we shall never understand our present difficulties unless we realize that war rates of wages and shorter hours of work, and the more expensive standards of living created by those rates of wages and that increased leisure, are just as much promisory notes and have just as little real wealth behind them.

Consequently, immediately after the war every nation plunged hastily head over ears into a renewed competition to sell the maximum quantity of mass-produced goods in all the markets of the world. The war did not in the least solve the dead-lock of which we were all so conscious before the war; on the contrary, it intensified it. Not only did every nation feel that large-scale production and trading offered them the only chance of redeeming all the promissory notes they had issued in the form of national debts and war wages, but there were more self-conscious nations in the field and the war had greatly stimulated their capacity for mass production.

The great criticism of the Peace of Versailles, a criticism which one seldom hears because one can-not blame any particular statesman for it, is that it completed the nationalist movement in Europe and established a number of new nations, like Czechoslovakia and Poland, each as intent as Ger-many and Italy had been in the last quarter of the nineteenth century, and even more so, on organizing themselves for industrial competition in the markets of the world.

At the same time, war conditions in industry had accustomed the older industrial nations to think in terms of mass production as never before. Moreover, the war has intensified the fall in the birth-rate (except during the year or two immediately suc-ceeding the armistice) and in this and other ways has cramped the consuming power of the markets for which all nations are competing.

We all know what the result has been. We have failed to redeem our promissory notes. The payment of interest on our national debts has absorbed an enormous proportion of our national revenues; the payment of war rates of wages has been more than our industries can support. Hence our unemployment. And as rates of wages have been reduced there has arisen an intense renewal of the old demand for a redistribution of wealth by taxation. But the attempts which have been made during the last seven years or so to meet this demand have, as we are now beginning to realize, only resulted in the issue of a new set of promissory notes, based not on present wealth but on future hopes, and the crisis through which we are now passing simply means that these notes have been presented for payment and we cannot pay.

I have ventured to give this very rough sketch of our post-war economic condition because I am anxious to direct attention to the root causes of that condition, rather than to temporary influences which have made that condition worse than it need have been. It is quite true that inter-Allied debts and German reparations have been so many monkey-wrenches thrown into the wheels of post-war industry by unwise statesmen; it is quite true that we look to statesmen to-day to set these mistakes right. But here, again, we are too apt to blame all our troubles on such things because we can find particular people whom we can accuse of being responsible for them. Our root troubles are those which we often overlook because we are all of us responsible for them—responsible by reason of our whole way of thought and our whole way of life. It was clearly very foolish of statesmen just after the war, when all nations were already up to the neck in a snowdrift of promissory notes, to pile up a new snowdrift of promissory notes from Germany to the Allies and from all the Allies to the United States, all of which would have to be redeemed somehow out of the future trade of the world. But even if our statesmen had been ideally wise, we should still have had to deal with the promissory notes which each nation had issued to its own people during the war itself, and it is these notes that we have found ourselves unable to redeem.

This is a gloomy picture of the post-war world, but just as I asked you not to underrate the very real improvement in social conditions during the nineteenth century, so I ask you particularly not to underrate the enormous benefits conferred on the country by the changes that have taken place since 1914. A friend of mine who used before the war to be in intimate contact with conditions in our great cities and who visited England last year for the first time since the war, summed up his impressions by telling me that there was no longer any poverty in Great Britain. That is an exaggeration, but the very fact that there are so few signs of poverty *on the surface* in this country to-day marks a revolutionary change.

And I do not chink I am far wrong in ascribing this improvement mainly to increased wages. Better education, better social services, have no doubt greatly helped; but you will observe that most of these forms of public assistance only give people temporary help restricted to their immediate needs. Temporary help of this kind can never enable people really to raise their standard of living, for an improved standard of living means that people are able to look further ahead and plan their lives on the assumption that they will have more to spend for some time to come.

Moreover, if you look beneath the surface of the social services I think you will be struck by the fact that they have often been created by a demand which would never have existed apart from increased wages. I am sure that this is true, for instance, of our infant welfare centres. It was the mothers with a little more money to spend on their babies and anxious for advice as to how best to spend that money on better feeding and so on who flocked to these centres after the war. It was certainly the greater spending power of the dweller in the villages which has made possible the success of that extraordinary movement, the Women's Institutes, which have transformed village life with no aid from the State. The whole political problem of the present day is how to maintain and increase this greater spending power of the mass of our population, in spite of the fact that it is based so largely on promissory notes, not on real present wealth.

In order to deal with that political problem we have in this country, under the influence of the war, also carried to its logical conclusion the principle of democracy and popular government. I am not sure that there was much more popular demand behind the great Suffrage Acts of 1918 and 1927 than there was behind the Acts of 1867 and 1885 —there may have been even less; I think we simply felt that there was no longer any logical argument against universal suffrage and that we might just as well finish the job while we were about it. And so, in this as in all other matters, we have now carried out the full implications of the old nineteenth-century gospel; we have gone with it as far as it will go.

Before asking you to consider the opinions of various people as to what we should do next, I would ask you to look back at what modern democracy, as the nineteenth century created it and the twentieth-century has completed it, has meant and done for the world.

Professor Trevelyan, at the end of his *History of England*, contrasts the England of the Napoleonic Wars with the England of the Great War. "Pitt and Castlereagh," he says, "fought the French as constitutional statesmen, by and through the House of Commons; but it never occurred to them or to any of their colleagues that the common people required, in time of national peril, any management or consideration beyond anti-Jacobin repression and the silencing of Parliamentary Reformers. . . . But the English Cabinet Ministers of 1914–1918 had always to appeal deferentially to the people. . . . The hardships of wartime did not, as a hundred years before, fall with the greatest force on the fortunes of the wage-earner. So long as the common danger of the war lasted the spirit of brotherhood in the British people of all classes, both at home and in the field, was at any rate much deeper and more widely spread than during the wars against Napoleon." All this is true and is to be placed to the credit of what we call democracy.

And yet—look at the end of the war, as compared with the end of the Napoleonic wars. Who were the wiser, the more humane—the statesmen placed in power by the mass of the people of this country at the General Election of 1918, or the Duke of Wellington, labouring at Paris in 1815 to prevent a vindictive peace and trying to end the armed occupation of French territory at the earliest possible moment?

Is not the truth this: that the great danger of democracy lies in the fact that it fosters and gives expression to mass movements of opinion at particular moments which sweep statesmen off their feet? Or rather, the danger is that the people who hold political power, whether they are a few aristocrats or all the men and women of a nation, must be organized if they are to use their power effectively, and that the more people you have to organize for this purpose, the more rigid the organization has to be and the more power you give to the organizer. Yet at the same time the organizer can only use his power in a rough sort of way, because of the numbers of men he has to move about. A brigade can march where it wants under a commander of its own choosing, but no commander, however chosen, can make it do folk-dancing or play Association football. As democracy grows and our civilization becomes more complicated, the danger is that we are using blunter and heavier tools to do finer and finer work. These considerations lead me to one or two things I should like to say about Mr. Woolf's talks about democracy.

With all respect, I think that Mr. Woolf confuses what democracy is with the things that he would like democracies to do. He would like democracy to promote the happiness and freedom of the individual and to give him equality of opportunity, mainly through education. Therefore he says that these things are democracy. But democracy is a form of government. It is that form of government where the rulers who actually conduct the government at any given moment are chosen by the mass of the people. At least that is what democracy means in great modern States where the mass of the people cannot individually take turns at govern-

ing as they used to do in a small Greek city like
Athens. And I am afraid it is rather difficult to
prove that the things that Mr. Woolf wants democracies to do are the things that democracies usually
do and that other forms of government usually fail
to do.

I have already indicated that I think the Duke
of Wellington was guided by the ideal of individual
human happiness in 1815 far more really than the
average French deputy or English member of Parliament in 1919. I am quite sure that the great
autocratic reformers in Europe in the last half of
the eighteenth century—men like Leopold of Tus-
cany and Pombal in Portugal—were more truly
inspired by that ideal than any democratic statesman of the nineteenth century. As to equality of
opportunity, Napoleon realized the ideal of a career
open to talent better than many democracies have
done. In education especially it is not very easy to
make out a case for democratic government. If you
read *Martin Chuzzlewit* you will see that Dickens
in 1840 did not think that the United States had
done as much for education as some European
monarchies. Scottish education certainly secured
more real equality of opportunity before Scotland
had a democratic form of government than it has
ever done since. Bismarck's Germany educated the
masses much more effectively than Gladstone's
England; and even anti-Fascists would admit how
great a reform Mussolini has brought about in

popular education in Italy. As a matter of fact I think education has very little to do with political democracy. I cannot respond to Mr. Woolf's and Mr. Tawney's challenge to name an Anglican bishop in recent years who was the son of working-class parents, but I could name a son of Italian working-class parents who became Bishop of Rome less than thirty years ago. This does not mean that Italy at that time was more democratic than England or had a better educational system. It simply means that the Roman Catholic Church is a very different kind of organization from the Church of England.

I think that my difference with Mr. Woolf comes out most clearly in his statement that democracy has not yet succeeded in the struggle against economic forces tending to make human society like a beehive. If that refers to the modern democracies of the last hundred years it seems to me like saying that the coach of the Cambridge Eight has not yet succeeded in the struggle against the tendency of the whole crew to row the same stroke. The whole of modern democracy seems to me to have been inextricably bound up with the effort to organize men in great communal labour forces for the mass production of wealth.

And so I come back to what I have said before. The great thing for us to consider is, not what democracy may do under certain conditions or what it has done under certain conditions in other ages, or what we should like it to do, but what the democracies of the modern world, of which we are members, have been doing and are doing to-day, and what they are likely to be able to do in the future. A peasant democracy in the Basque provinces of northern Spain in the fourteenth century or in Esthonia to-day will act very differently from a city democracy like ancient Athens or mediaeval Hamburg; and both will act very differently from a national industrial democracy like modern England. The question we must ask is: What prospect have we of using our modern industrial democracy to overcome the difficulties in which the modern world is involved?

I HAVE tried to show that the social ideals which have dominated the growth of our modern democracy have been one-sided and that they have led us into a blind alley. It has been pointed out to me that the end of this blind alley was foreseen by Socialists in the nineteenth century. "General prosperity in a country under a capitalist régime," to quote from the old Social Democratic Federation, "depends not on the amount of wealth within the country, but on its ability to dispose of its surplus wealth. Hence, when all countries are fully capitalized and there are no fields for exploitation, no country will be able to dispose of its surplus wealth and the capitalist system will crack. Capitalism therefore contains within itself the seeds of its own destruction."

This seems to me to be a fairly accurate forecast of what has actually happened. But it seems to me equally clear that it has not happened because capital has been in private hands instead of in the hands of the State. It has happened because we have tried rapidly to increase our wealth by extreme division of labour, and this has, in practice, been the Socialist as well as the individualist ideal. Any country which tries to raise its standard of living by producing more manufactured goods than it can consume, in order that it may buy cheaply from other countries the goods and clothing materials which it needs, must inevitably come up against this limitation, sooner or later.

The question for us now is, Can we break away from this old one-sided political philosophy? Can we make a fresh start?

I think everyone will admit that we are finding it very difficult to-day to make a fresh start. I have referred to the unwieldiness of political movements in a modern democracy and I now want to pursue this idea a little further.

Both in politics and in industry, and, indeed, in every activity of our life to-day, we seem only to be able to get things done by belonging to associations which are more or less highly organized. In politics, one of the most clearly marked features of democracy is that the larger the number of voters the more highly organized do political parties tend to become. This tendency can best be studied in the United States. The American "political boss" has become a by-word. The whole of American politics, for some years before the war, and, indeed, even earlier, centred round an effort to diminish the power of political organizations, but the effort was not very successful. Our danger in this country is that, because the management of our political parties has been, let us say, more respectable than in the United States, we do not realize that our political life has been developing in the same direction. The result of this elaborate organization of parties is to discourage novelty and initiative; it puts a premium upon what the Americans call "the available man," that is to say, the man who is regarded as "safe," who has no inconvenient originality, who treads on the fewest number of toes.

In the older parties, Conservative and Liberal, this kind of discouragement of initiative does not, perhaps, take the form of any personal coercion of parliamentary candidates or members of Parliament. On the whole, the Liberal or Conservative member of Parliament is given a pretty free hand by his local political associations and by his central party machine. His initiative is discouraged rather by the dead-weight of the ordinary party views to which the party machine feels obliged to confine itself in its political propaganda in order not to shock any of its supporters. The individual politician can speak his own mind, but his voice is smothered by the official voice of the party machine.

In the Labour Party, so far as I can judge, there is much less personal freedom, simply because the Labour Party has been, throughout its whole history, the attacking party, and it has therefore been more necessary for it to maintain unity and ensure that all its members are keeping step. It could never have had the phenomenal success which it has enjoyed but for this high degree of discipline. On the other hand, the official Labour Party machine is much less cautious in its propaganda than that of the older parties and is more ready to voice original views. But, though parties may thus differ from each other in the precise way in which they discourage initiative, the result with all of them is pretty much the same.

The same thing is, of course, true of the trade unions which have played such a large part in building up the Labour Party. But here we come up against another element in the problem. There is always a pretty definite limit to the organization of political parties because, after all, the duty of a member of Parliament is a duty to the electorate and not to his party machine, and it has been proved over and over again in all parties that a politician of courage can successfully appeal to the electorate against his party machine. But in a trade union, the duty of a trade union official is to the members of the union and to the members of the union alone. In wage negotiations, his duty is to get the best possible wages for his members, not to consider the interests of the industry as a whole, though, of course, he will recognize that if the industry is not prosperous it cannot pay good wages. He is an advocate of the workers' point of view; not a judge of what is best for the industry.

I can explain what I mean best by taking a concrete instance, not of a trade union but of a professional union. The National Union of Teachers is one of the most public-spirited organizations in the country. For the last few years, at any rate, its whole attention has been concentrated upon improving the education of the people. But, when it comes to salary negotiations, the duty of the officials who represent the Union on the Burnham Committees is to maintain at least the present rate of salaries of its members, and it is very doubtful whether any of those officials can reconcile it with his duty, in any circumstances, to agree, of his own volition, to a reduction in the rate of salary of any section of his members. Much the same thing is true of those members of the Burnham Committee who represent the local authorities of the country; and that is why the Burnham Committees so often reach a deadlock in their negotiations.

I have taken this instance in order to indicate that all professional associations and all associations of public authorities tend to share with trade unions this characteristic of extreme rigidity and absence of initiative. It is a grave question whether any officer of any such association can be public-spirited in the best sense without failing in his duty to those whom he is elected to represent. That means that the whole of our social life tends to be organized into big combinations of men whose official business it is only to see one side of a public question or, at least, only to argue one side of such a question. Each such combination tends to behave like an ostrich, burying its head in the sand and proclaiming that its own particular patch of sand is the only patch where any self-respecting bird will lay its head.

And the same criticism applies to organizations of capital. Quite certainly modern society could never have increased its wealth and raised the standard of living of all its members, as it has done, if it had not been for the limited liability company. But it is equally true that, as the big limited liability company, financed by the savings of an enormous number of comparatively small shareholders, has replaced the old family or private business, it has increasingly become the duty of the directors of industry to look after the immediate interests of their shareholders rather than the ultimate prosperity of their business.

In modern society everything depends upon organized industry. Organized industry is not only the agent for the protection of wealth, it is also, and must always be, the main agent for the distribution of wealth. The amount of national wealth distributed by social services must always be a drop in the ocean compared with the amount distributed in the form of wages and interest. If the managers of industry are to any extent estopped from being public-spirited by the duty which they owe to the shareholders who have elected them, then our whole national economy is likely to go desperately wrong.

I could continue to give other instances of the same tendency. For example, even the small capitalist to-day tends to invest his money in industry, not according to his personal choice and judgment, but through some Investment Trust company who undertakes to invest his money for him. But I have said enough to indicate what seems to me to be the great disability under which modern democratic society is labouring at this crisis of its fate. Every phase of our life tends to be organized on the democratic representative principle. We are all electing various people, company directors, trade union officials as well as local municipal councillors and members of Parliament, to look after this or that section of our interests; and all this apparatus of representative organization tends to result in mental petrifaction. We do not think for ourselves, because we have elected people to think for us; and the people we have elected to think for us dare not, for that very reason, think for themselves. This is the vicious circle in which we are all involved.

It is often suggested that democracy would have worked better if we had educated the people beforehand; many people feel that our democracy has gone wrong because compulsory education was started far too late. There may be something in this view; yet, on the other hand, I do not think we should ever have become dominated by organized associations, as we are to-day, unless we had been educated up to it. Hard as our teachers strive against the standardization of education, almost every system of popular education I know of in industrial countries—in America, in Germany, in Fascist Italy, and in our own country—tends to produce a more or less standardized type of mind. Or rather, it tends to accentuate the standardizing influence exerted by social conditions in big industrial centres of population. One of the things required of Russian school children of twelve or fourteen is that they shall have been taught "community abilities" such as the ability to take part in and lead clubs and committees; and I sometimes fear that Soviet Russia is only demonstrating to us all the tendency of every industrial civilization. Education cannot cope with a wrong social atmosphere.

Because of the wrong social atmosphere into which we have drifted, present-day politics tends to take the form of continual attempts to patch up temporary compromises between rigidly organized interests and rigidly limited minds. We all know this in the political life of this nation. Wage negotiations between trade unions and employers' federations are always temporary compromises. So are similar negotiations between the State, on the one hand, and civil servants or teachers, on the other. Nearly all the legislation of Parliament for the last ten years has taken the form of compromises of this kind. The Rent Restrictions Acts, for instance, have been mere temporary patchwork which everyone knows cannot last indefinitely.

We sometimes try to explain this political immobility by saying that the facts of modern industrial civilization have become so complex that anything one tries to do has repercussions in all sorts of unexpected directions. But when we say this, we really mean that we are dealing with large bodies of men with divergent interests, and that the Government, in spite of all the improved methods of publicity which it has at its disposal nowadays, is unable to get agreement between these bodies to work on a particular plan.

Perhaps the most striking instance of this compromise habit to which we are condemned is the League of Nations.

In the early days of the League, I once praised it on the ground that it was an unassuming attempt to realize in international affairs the old principle of "the greatest good of the greatest number"—that its business was not to try to set up some supreme International Government, but to try to adjust conflicting national interests and smooth over international frictions "by the display of a charity which may yet avail to cover the multitude of our sins." I still think this. I think the League of Nations has more than fully justified the hopes of its founders, and that if it had tried to be more ambitious the world might well be even less peaceful than it is to-day.

But we should be very blind if we did not realize that the League of Nations can seldom really solve any great problem. The nations of the world are more highly organized and more self-conscious, as nations, than ever before. Their representatives on the League of Nations have far less freedom to make agreements. No democratic statesman, elected to protect national interests and responsible to a parliamentary majority in the House of Commons or the French Chamber of Deputies or the German Reichstag, feels himself free to sacrifice some relatively unimportant national interest for the sake of some ultimate aim of policy as Wellington or Castlereagh were free one hundred years ago. After the Napoleonic wars we forgave our Allies their debts to us on a scale of which we have never dreamt in the last ten years. We sometimes think we have founded the League of Nations because we are more internationally-minded than our forefathers. The truth is that, owing to our democratic national organization, we are so much less internationally-minded than our forefathers that the world simply could not get along unless it had an organized League of Nations to secure some sort of adjustment of national interests. But in such a world these adjustments are bound to be mere temporary compromises.

This is a very dark picture of the modern world, and, no doubt, it is exaggerated. One cannot examine things properly unless one puts them under a microscope and magnifies them a little. In view of recent events I should be the last to deny that a democratic electorate can, on occasion, give its leaders a free hand. But I know of no other democracy than Great Britain where an election could conceivably have the result of the late election in this country.

The strength of the British democracy is, in fact, that it has never quite learnt to regard itself as a democracy, and still assumes that the King's Ministers are something more than a committee of the legislature. We have therefore always encouraged our political leaders to lead, though usually with very little success.

Broadly speaking, in spite of the good sense and good feeling often shown by democratic electorates, I am afraid it is true that although society to-day is faced with bigger problems and bigger dangers than ever before, it is less well equipped than ever before to deal with them. And I think it is also true that this weakness is mainly due to the fact that nearly all the members of society are either being represented by somebody or are representing somebody else, and that, consequently, few of them are able to think for themselves and still fewer have the courage to say and to act upon what they think. In fact, I am almost inclined to say that I do not know what would have happened to this country if it had not been for woman's suffrage, because women are, for the most part, individualists and do not think and vote as members of rigidly organized associations. If women ever copy men in this respect, I think our democracy will, indeed, become impossible.

It is these facts that have, I think, mainly led to the modern revolt against democracy.

THE revolt against modern industrial democracy is not a revolt against all that ideal conception of democracy which Mr. Woolf discussed, nor is it a revolt which can be understood by anyone who persists in using the old phraseology of nineteenth-century political and economic controversies. Many people seem unable to get away from phrases about "private enterprise" and "capitalist system." All these phrases seem to me to be good for nothing except to prevent people from thinking. The revolt which we have to consider is really, more than anything else, a revolt against this muddled thinking. It is an attempt to get back to realities—an attempt which was, of course, the real driving force behind the original Socialist movement, and which remains the driving force behind that movement as it is now manifested in the Soviet Republic.

But Socialism in Western Europe has become as much an affair of compromises and confused thinking as older political schools of thought. I remember twenty years ago being exasperated by two sentences in Lord Snowden's book *Socialism and Syndicalism*. These two sentences were: "Some people fear the power of what they call officialism or bureaucracy under Socialism. Socialism will be democratic: the people will rule." That seemed to me then and seems to me still to be shirking the real problem of government by the use of a phrase. It ignores the great difficulty: the unreality of nine-tenths of our efforts to get our best thoughts and desires represented by the men whom we elect to manage our business for us.

And on the top of this muddled thinking we have to contend with a great deal of thinking which is sound enough in its way but which never seems to lead anywhere. Much of modern discontent about the relative rewards that come to the wage-earner on the one hand and the owner of capital on the other seems to me to come within this description. It is always quite easy to make any social system look silly, because every social system is illogical; but this is a futile amusement unless you yourself are prepared to follow your own line of criticism to its logical conclusion. For instance, I remember the late Mr. Wheatley, when he was Minister of Health, pointing out that the high cost of building houses to let to working men was due, not to the cost of wages, but to the cost of interest. That is quite true, but think what it means. It means that if the workmen who build a house were prepared to "invest" their labour, i.e. to spread the payment for their labour over a number of years, taking it out of the annual rent paid by the tenant, they would not need the help of any capitalist. Moreover, if they were prepared to charge nothing to the tenant for his delay (so to speak) in paying their wages—i.e. if they charged no interest on the investment of their labour—the rent the tenant would have to pay would be lower. But is this actually what the bricklayer wants to do?

Can anyone wonder that a crowded world in desperate trouble, finding that every attempt it makes to set its house in order is blocked by muddled thinking or by arguments which go round and round in a circle, tries sometimes to get rid of the obstacle by some kind of dictatorship? Perhaps I am being rather unfair to Lord Snowden and Mr. Wheatley, but, if so, I am only faithfully representing the kind of impatience which has produced Mussolini.

But mere impatience never did any good in this world, and that is why so many attempts during the last few years to imitate Mussolini in other countries have ended in fiasco. We are far too apt to talk about this revolt against democracy as if it was likely to take the same form in every country. The first thing to understand about Fascism is that, in a sense, it is not a new thing in Italy, but has its roots very deep in Italian character and history. Italian politics, in past centuries, have often taken the form of the dictatorship of a party, and, in one aspect, Fascism is only this old tradition breaking up through a thin layer of parliamentary institutions which have been, as it were, superimposed on Italian life during the last sixty or seventy years.

These institutions had failed to discharge some of the elementary duties of all political institutions.

They had failed to secure law and order and clean government; above all, they had failed in the chief work they were set seventy years ago—the task of making "United Italy" a really united nation. Naples and Lombardy and Central Italy were, as it were, only loosely sewn together, not fused into a union. In that sense—judged by those practical standards—Italian democracy had failed. The Fascist Party does not therefore represent a crude experiment in imperialism, nor merely a return to old tradition, an impatient revolt against unrealities, or a desire to get down to facts, to act instead of talking. It also represents a very real and a very high ideal of social action, community spirit and national unity of which Italy, owing to her peculiar history and conditions, stood in peculiar need.

In Germany, again, so far as I can judge, the revolt against democracy embodied in the Hitler Party is in some measure a revival of the old German alliance between a dominant army or military movement and a more or less subordinate political machine. I fancy it would be true to say that, at the start, Hitlerism was an imitation of Fascism, but that so long as it was a mere imitation it met with very little success. Since then it has increasingly taken a form which represents an old German tradition and has become profoundly modified in the process. Whether it will succeed or not largely depends on whether the German people have turned their back upon that old tradition or not.

Other attempted dictatorships—for instance, in Spain—seem to have failed pretty badly because they were merely imitations or opportunist attempts to deal with emergencies. They had no real roots in the country they sought to govern, consequently they were never able to build up a coherent body of political opinion to support them. Turkey is, of course, a different case which need not detain us. You cannot have a revolt against democracy in a country where no democracy has existed.

The same thing might be said of Russia, which has had no more practical experience of democracy than Turkey, but the Russian Communist experiment is something much more than a revolt against democracy; it is in the strictest sense a revolt against religion—against the whole system of faith and morals which has governed the mind of civilized men for some fifteen hundred years. We cannot begin to understand Russia unless we realize this. Other dictatorships, like Fascism, can be more or less explained as a mere effort to run a country efficiently—to make modern industrial civilization work. The Fascist would say that the preaching of freedom and emancipation was necessary in Mazzini's days, in the middle of the nineteenth century, but that to-day the preaching of discipline is equally necessary. He would regard himself as working to the same nationalist aim as Mazzini, using a somewhat different instrument. He has not sought to change the fundamental beliefs of his countrymen;

on the contrary, he has allied himself closely to the Catholic Church. The member of the Fascist Party may often be brutal in his methods, as Tammany in New York may be brutal; but he recognizes the same moral sanctions as those on which European Governments have always rested since the days of Constantine.

But to the Russian Communist Party these sanctions mean less than nothing. Such ideals as the promotion of individual human happiness do not enter into its calculations at all. The community is everything, a community which, beginning as a sort of elect body of saints wielding all political power, is eventually to embrace the whole human race. Russia, to-day, is a reminder, on a colossal scale, of an old truth which we are all too prone to forget. Let me emphasize this truth. A social system, based upon the worship of humanity, is the cruelest of all possible social systems, and the substitution of that worship for supernatural religion leads, paradoxically but inevitably, to inhumanity. That was the lesson of the Reign of Terror in the French Revolution and it is the lesson of the Russian Revolution too. I wish that some people to-day who talk of getting rid of supernatural religion would remember this. But intensely as we may dislike this denial of the whole system of morals by which Western Europe and America have lived for centuries, even when we have been most untrue to it, we miss the whole point if we ignore the burning idealism which is the real driving force behind the Soviet experiment. We have grown accustomed to think, during the last two or three years, that Soviet policy is represented by the industrial and commercial programme which is known as the Five-Year Plan. It is sometimes said that whether democracy survives or not depends entirely on whether the Five-Year Plan succeeds, with the inference that if it does so we shall all immediately adopt the Soviet system. The Five-Year Plan is simply an effort to acquire for the Soviet Government the wealth necessary to enable it to carry out its policy rapidly. If it fails no doubt the people of Russia, whose energies have been so exclusively concentrated on the Plan, would be gravely disillusioned and that might endanger the stability of the Soviet Government, but I think the great mass of the Communist Party in Russia would regard it merely as a temporary set-back. It would probably not have anything like the same effect as an economic breakdown in Italy might have on the prestige of the Fascist Party. The ideal of the International Revolution in which every Russian child is being deliberately educated to the exclusion of all other thoughts and beliefs would survive such a disappointment as it has survived so many sufferings which the Russian people have undergone during the last ten years.

This is, of course, a very inadequate summary of the revolt against democracy, but it is perhaps sufficient to form a basis for the question we have to answer, namely: whether these experiments in dictatorship offer any better prospect of the fresh start, which we all want in politics, than the parliamentary democracy whose drawbacks I have discussed.

The answer I think is: No. Except in the case of Russia, these experiments are not as new as they look; they are to some extent a return to older traditions of government peculiar to the countries concerned. But, besides this, their main characteristic—and this applies to Russia above all—is that they are attempts to build a bigger structure on the old nineteenth-century philosophy of which I have said so much in these talks. We go wrong because we confuse that philosophy itself with the temporary arrangements which our grandfathers thought were best adapted to put it into practice. They believed, it is true, in what I have elsewhere called the Bo-peep Doctrine—the idea that if every individual was allowed by the State to set about making money according to his own best judgment all the citizens of a country would eventually come home bringing social welfare with them. But this individualism changed gradually and naturally into collectivism as soon as it became evident that social welfare did not, in fact, come about automatically in quite this way. Our trouble has been that, having mobilized and concentrated the great industrial armies which make up the modern

State—and believing, as we still do, that the modern State cannot exist except by keeping these armies mobilized—we have never quite had the courage to treat our industrial armies as military armies have always been treated—to bring them under discipline. Yet our industrial armies to-day, engaged in making things that they cannot consume, are almost as little self-supporting as a military army and need almost as much a system of discipline and a Government-managed commissariat. These foreign dictatorships, accepting the necessity for a national or international mobilization of this kind, have simply had the courage to draw the logical conclusion from these premises. Having to handle a society where comparatively few individuals can be really free, because they cannot be even approximately self-supporting, they have frankly discarded freedom as a political principle.

Russia has, of course, gone much further. The Russian Communist has not only accepted the philosophy in which we have really believed, the things we really took for granted, and discarded the political principles to which we have only given lip service—like freedom; he has also substituted for the religion which we still profess, but with which in his view our industrial civilization is incompatible, a religion which he would say represents much more nearly our actual industrial practice. Do not think that I share this view about the unreality of our religious professions. I am not a cynic of that kind, and, in fact, I regard this Communist religion as the supreme error which Christianity has to overcome. But it is the supreme error precisely because it is the logical exaggeration of many errors in which, for the last hundred years and more, Christianity has too often indolently acquiesced.

For those, then, who are prepared fatalistically to remain bound to the chariot of what I may call the Industrial State, these foreign dictatorships may offer a temporary solution of some of our most urgent problems, if that is the best we can do and if we have the courage to do it. But to those who are not content to remain thus bound and who want a fresh start towards some better political and social ideal, however long and difficult the road may be, I cannot see that these dictatorships offer any lesson, except one—the old lesson that no society can survive unless every citizen is prepared to make definite sacrifices to maintain it.

Fundamentally, this appeal to sacrifice is the driving force behind every one of these systems of dictatorship. And they all remind us that in this one respect, at any rate, the radical economists of the nineteenth century were wrong; that the appeal of society to its members must not be an appeal to their enlightened self-interest, but an appeal to their power of sacrifice.

There is, however, one particular experiment in Italy from which I believe we can·learn much— the experiment that goes by the name of the "Corporative State." In Italy this experiment is based on two principles: that no body of men, employers or employed, have the right to stop work, since it is on their organized work that the welfare of the State depends; and that all associations of workmen and employers, if formed according to broad rules laid down by the State, have the right and duty to advise the State on industrial matters through their authorized representatives. The first principle leads to the legal prohibition of strikes and lockouts and to the control by the State of the processes of collective bargaining, and the second has led to the establishment of a representative "Council of Corporations" as a sort of industrial Parliament.

But there is something else that we ought to learn from those dictatorships, and that is that the appeal to sacrifice must not be exaggerated. You cannot keep men's energies screwed up beyond a certain point for an indefinite period; their nerves will snap, the reaction will come. This simple fact is likely to prove the undoing of all these dictatorships, unless they invent means to make their administration more flexible than it is at the present moment. Inflexibility is the weakness of dictatorships; a temporary dictatorship is the most difficult thing in the world to establish, because the very methods which make dictatorships useful make it almost impossible to terminate them and to return to more ordinary methods.

And this seems to me to be the supreme virtue

of parliamentary government: that it provides a constant thermometer of the moral temperature of society and a thermometer attached, as it were, to a self-regulating furnace which can adjust itself to the rise and fall in temperature. Whatever we may feel about that vague word Democracy, let us beware that we do not sacrifice this enormous advantage which any dictatorship would give much to possess.

12. OUR PROBLEM TO-DAY

I MUST now try to reach some sort of conclusion about what modern industrial democracies can do and what they must do if they are to survive. I must not, as a politician, try to lay down the political programme in which I believe, nor discuss what I would do with the world. I propose only to try to indicate the sort of spirit in which I think we ought to approach our present-day problems.

And, to begin with, let us approach our problems with confidence. One of the worst results of what I have called "living in crowds" is that it breeds what modern psychologists call an "inferiority complex." I have been trying to overcome this inferiority complex by tracing our ills to their real cause, that is, to a certain state of mind. You may think that I have been depressing and pessimistic—but the real pessimist is a man who takes our modern state of mind—what I have called our nineteenth-century philosophy—for granted, and then criticizes everything that modern society does—saying, for instance, that our workmen do not work, that our education is bad, that our health services are extravagant, that the managers of industry are inefficient, and so on. Most of this is nonsense. We have a great deal to learn from foreign countries both in industry and in social services; we have got to be energetic and drastic in our reforms in many directions; in many matters we have got to plan our industrial life much more scientifically; but I should say that, so far from being, broadly speaking, less well equipped than other countries to solve our problems, we are, on the whole, better equipped than any of them.

The British workman, owing to his comparatively high standard of living, used always to be the most efficient workman in the world. Other countries may have out-distanced us, for the moment, in technical and art education for the training of skilled workmen in this or that branch of industry, but, on the other hand, the physical health of the mass of our population, and consequently their physical efficiency, have been greatly improved during the last thirty years, partly owing to the school medical and infant welfare services which grew up after the South African War and after the Great War respectively. This improvement has maintained and even increased our lead. The managers of our industries, though in many cases they may have got into a groove, are proving once more, up and down the country to-day, that when they set their mind to the re-planning of their businesses, they can, in co-operation with their workmen, compete successfully with foreign industries in spite of the higher wages and higher standards of living of this country. What we in this country need to do, we can do, if we will set our mind to it. It is only our state of mind that has been wrong.

And now what do we need to do? In the first place we have to redeem our promissory notes. Not only, nor chiefly, the money we borrowed to make shells in the war, but, far more, the higher standards of wages and leisure which we set up during the war, relying on a future prosperity which has not yet come to us. If we set about our task in the right spirit we shall rapidly reduce the comparatively small burden represented by our war debts, for we shall be able to reduce the rate of interest upon them through conversion operations. But on the other and far greater volume of promissory notes, represented by higher wages and shorter hours of work, we must try, as it were, to pay both the principal and the full rate of interest. That means, in practice, that for this purpose we must go on and press forward with the old nineteenth-century idea of the development of foreign markets,

I began by reminding you of the importance of judgment in political matters. It is quite true that this nineteenth-century idea was one-sided, and that by exaggerating it we have plunged ourselves into a deadlock of competition which is a danger not only to the prosperity, but also to the peace of the world. But, within its proper limits, the idea is sound. The present industrial depression, which prevents us from paying our promissory notes, is at the same time preventing countries like the South American countries, which have been great markets for our goods in the past, from continuing their development and thus redeeming the promissory notes which they, in their turn, had issued in reliance upon their future development. The same is true of countries belonging to our own Empire, like Australia. It is right, therefore, and urgently necessary, that we should energetically reorganize and re-plan our production for the purpose of efficient competition in foreign markets.

It is here, I think, that we have much to learn from the Fascist idea of the "Corporative State." As I have already said, one of our chief weaknesses to-day is that it is difficult for trade unions or employers' federations to be public-spirited in the best sense. We ought, as it were, to steady associations of workmen and employers by giving them definite duties to perform for the State. I do not believe in the State trying to run industry, but, on the other hand, it seems to me absolutely wrong that you should have within the framework of our society so powerful an organization as (let us say) the Trade Union Congress, without giving it any definite responsibilities towards the community or any definite duties to the community. It is only the Government that can define the responsibilities and duties of a powerful organization like this to the community, and I think it should be possible to define them in such a way as not to involve State interference with the freedom either of workmen or employers.

For example, the State cannot run the building

industry, and our experiment of subsidizing that industry has not been a success; but I think the State has a right to require the building industry so to organize itself that it can build working-class houses without subsidies. The first step in this direction is probably to place upon all associations of workmen and employers the definite responsibility for advising the State on matters affecting industry through some such body as the Council of Corporations established by Mussolini in Italy. I would ask you to consider the idea. Parliamentary government (I prefer that word to democracy) can survive if it does what it portends to dò—namely, to represent the nation. At present it does not properly represent, in this country, either employers' or workers' organizations or industry. It ought to be made to do so as soon as possible.

But now we come to the other side of our task—that other side which the one-sided ideas of the nineteenth century ignored. Foreign trade, the development of foreign markets, is not the main aim of social policy. The main aim of our social policy in England is, so to speak, to make good homes for Englishmen—for the individual men and women who are citizens of this country. And the work by which the individual gets his living or the career which is open to him in the course of his work, is not really the main thing in anyone's life. The purpose of all work is to enable the individual to live his own life outside his work and, if he is public spirited and in proportion to his abilities and opportunities, to help other individuals to live their own lives outside their work.

What the whole nineteenth-century philosophy tended to miss was this idea of the intensive cultivation, as it were, of our own home country so as to provide within it the greatest possible variety of opportunities for individuals to follow their own tastes and live the sort of life they want to live. This becomes all the more important at the present day when the chances of emigration are so much restricted and when the man who (for instance) would rather be a small farmer than a dock labourer cannot follow his tastes by finding a farm in Canada.

What direction might an intensive cultivation of our home land take?

In the first place I think no society can give its citizens a sense of freedom and variety of opportunity unless it is far less dependent than we in England are upon foreign countries for the necessaries of life. Let me put two pictures before you. Go through Brittany and Normandy from Brest to Havre, cross to Southampton and go up the Portsmouth Road to Guildford. On one side of the Channel you will see intense cultivation of the land by a peasant population, often very poor, but obviously with a home life and a simple culture of their own. On the other side you will get an impression of a richer countryside (richer than Brittany at any rate) turned into a sort of teagarden for motorists and suburban dwellers from London. Or again, go through Durham and you will get an impression of an intense industrial development interspersed with green fields showing no corresponding development of the soil to meet the immediate needs of this crowded population. This means that the population eats bacon and butter from Denmark and does not eat any green vegetables at all. Of course I am exaggerating, but not very much. Never did any country have such an opportunity as we have had to intersperse our mines and factories with intense cultivation of the soil for a market next door; never has any country had such an opportunity to breed an industrial population living partly on the land and partly in the factory; and never has any country so neglected its opportunities. We have dismissed this whole problem by a few easy catchwords about "Protection" and "No Food Taxes." Depend upon it, a nation which lives, like Imperial Rome, on food ships from overseas, will, sooner or later, experience the same moral decay as Imperial Rome. Let us realize that since the war we have, to a very considerable extent, already split up the ownership of land. Perhaps our main business to-day is to make use of the opportunity which this wider distribution of land has already put into our hands.

My second suggestion is this—that in education and in our whole outlook on life we need to substitute, to a very considerable extent, the idea of craftsmanship for the ideal of "getting on." We have got a far better system of technical education in this country than we give ourselves credit for, but it grew up in the nineteenth century along nineteenth-century lines: that is to say, it aims mainly at teaching the scientific principles on which industrial processes rest, for the purpose of helping the workman to rise to positions of management. It assumes that actual skill in industrial processes will be taught in the workshop itself. But nowadays the workman's son who is likely to rise to positions of management tends to go to the secondary school, and in many industries workshop teaching is not what it used to be. It is, I believe, a profound, though a very common, mistake to suppose that skill in workmanship is being crowded out by modern mass-production methods. Countries like France and Czechoslovakia seem to be now making an energetic effort to cultivate in their industrial workers the same kind of self-reliance based on skill as has characterized their agricultural populations of peasant proprietors, and this is a lesson we may well learn from them.

But let us be clear about one thing: that this ideal of craftsmanship must apply to all classes of the population. I have suggested that we shall be wise to regard the function of our foreign trade as, roughly speaking, limited to the maintenance of our existing standard of material wealth—what I have called the redemption of our war-time promissory notes. I have suggested that for the rest we ought to concentrate mainly on giving our people at home wider opportunities of converting that wealth into better standards of living. But if this is the sort of prospect to which we have to look forward, then what we now call "the leisured classes" will tend to disappear.

There has already been a great change in this direction in the last thirty years. One of the clear lessons of history is that a leisured class based upon inherited wealth must be a class of landowners. Trading investments are always a very insecure foundation for such a class, and they will become increasingly insecure as the rate of the accumulation of wealth slows down. There is no longer such a thing as a landowning class in this country, and that means that in the future the distinctions between class and class will tend rapidly to diminish. All classes will increasingly have to rely on acquired skill as the only means of earning a living and, what is more important, the only means of securing an assured position in the community. We shall be a simpler, more strenuous, perhaps even a poorer community; but we shall realize that a high standard of wealth is not the same thing as a good standard of living, a good standard of comfort, or a good standard of culture. If we can succeed in making that obvious discovery, we shall have found what the nineteenth century missed.

At this point some of you may be inclined to say

"this man is a Little Englander." Well, in a sense perhaps I am. I agree with Mr. Woolf that we have to be, as never before, citizens of the world, because we are affected, more profoundly than ever before, by what goes on in foreign countries. But to a considerable extent we are so affected because, like the "fool" in Scripture, our "eyes have been on the ends of the earth" for a hundred years past, and we have neglected the cultivation of our own home garden. Relentless economic facts are driving us back to that neglected garden. We can choose between bowing to those facts or imitating the Communists of Russia who are sacrificing the happiness of at least two generations of Russians in an attempt to win international economic power. There is no other alternative. But if we do take up the cultivation of our own home garden, we may lead the way in a new international movement towards a system of international trade agreements based on the principles of self-support and mutual help, rather than on the principle of competition.

And with a view to giving the world such a lead, I should try first to set an example to the world by establishing such a system, based on such principles, in our own Empire. For I am an Imperialist as well as a Little Englander. But I am not an imperialist in Mr. Woolf's sense; no Englishman is. I said before that I thought Mr. Woolf was confusing what democracy is with the things he would like democracy to do. So, too, I think he is con-

fusing what imperialism is with certain things that
he does not want an empire to do. And in doing
so I think he has missed most of the real difficulties
of our imperial problems. He has said, for instance,
that, in each country of our Empire, we "should
think first and last of the everyday happiness of
the *ordinary person* and that the *population* should
enjoy complete political and social equality, and
should be encouraged to use *its* liberty and independence." You see, he changes in the middle of
his sentence from the *person* to the *population*; which
means that he rather light-heartedly assumes that
the ordinary Indian will be happier every day if
Indians as a nation are independent of the British
Parliament. He therefore misses the historical fact
that British imperial policy in Asia and Africa has
been, and is still to-day, a perpetual tug-of-war
between our responsibility for the everyday happiness of the individuals we rule and our belief in
the general desirability of self-government. I don't
believe for a moment that the two things are incompatible in the long run; but I agree with Mr.
Woolf that we ought to think "first and last" of
the everyday happiness of the ordinary person in
each country of the Empire, and I should try to
give *him*, the ordinary person (not *it*, the population),
the greatest possible sense of independence, precisely
as I wish to give that sense to the greatest possible
number of Englishmen and Scotsmen.

It is on that basis that I should like to come to

commercial agreements with each country of the Empire. For instance, my agreement with India would be based on a full recognition of the soundness of Mr. Gandhi's policy about what we in this country would call cottage industries. For depend upon it, democracy can only survive—in fact, it can only be born—if the "population" which rules is composed of individuals who are each ruling his or her own life. A nation cannot be politically independent if its citizens are, each of them, socially dependent; it cannot be self-governing if its citizens have no real opportunity, each of them, to govern his or her own way of living. That is what the nineteenth century forgot; that is what we have to remember.

Modern democracies are in danger to-day, as every form of human government has been in danger over and over again in the past, because they have been possessed by what a modern poet has called "a dumb devil of pride and greed." We shall not avert our danger by resorting to dictatorships which worship that devil as a god; but neither shall we avert it by talking about democracy as if it were a divine principle of life, instead of a mere piece of human organization which may go bad like any other invention of man. On the other hand, we may succeed in averting it if we rid ourselves of the old nineteenth-century one-sided passion for the pursuit of wealth and learn instead that attitude of mind indicated by Ruskin's epigram; "Care not much to make money, but care to make much of it."

One word in conclusion. While these talks were being broadcast I was urged to supply an alternative to that burning idealism which I referred to in speaking of Russian Communism. I can only repeat that the alternative lies in, supernatural religion. If I am asked, What is the relation of politics to supernatural religion? I can only reply by a quotation: "Thus saith the Lord, keep ye judgment, and do justice: for my salvation is near to come and my righteousness to be revealed." That quotation represents the supreme change of mind that the world needs.

PART II

SOCIAL INSTITUTIONS

MRS. SIDNEY WEBB

and

PROFESSOR W. G. S. ADAMS

MRS. SIDNEY WEBB

I. DISEASES OF ORGANIZED SOCIETY

1. THE NATURE AND CLASSIFICATION OF SOCIAL INSTITUTIONS

WHAT is a social institution; can we define it? It is clearly not a living organism in the sense that a plant, a dog, or a man is an organism. No one has ever seen or touched or smelt a social institution. No one has ever heard it speak or has spoken to it. Its existence cannot, in fact, be directly perceived; it can only be inferred by observing and reasoning about a lot of other things.

Let us take the most prominent of our social institutions, Parliament itself. If a foreigner came and asked me, "What is and where is your Parliament? Will you kindly show it to me?" I should answer, "Certainly, come and look at it." I should take him first to the gallery of the House of Commons. He would look down into a gloomy, badly-ventilated hall; and he would see, passing in and out, some hundreds of men and a few women. At times they might all be crowded together on the dull green benches, listening intently; or if there happen d to be an insignificant or dull-witted member speaking, they would be chattering among themselves, to the great discomfort and humiliation of the unheeded speaker. Then a bell would ring; they would all troop out, some to the right and some to the left. Maybe a few superior persons, who could not make up their minds which way they would vote, would retain their seats. Presently the crowd would surge in again, followed by four tellers, two for each side, who would walk solemnly up to the table, bow to the Speaker, and the two representing the winning side would read out amid cheers and jeers the number of "ayes" and "noes," respectively.

Then I would take my foreigner to the House of Lords. I would show him the Lord Chancellor in his wig and gown, seated uncomfortably on a red sack of wool without a back to it; on the scarlet benches to his right might be the two Archbishops and a score or so of Bishops in their lawn sleeves; the Government Peers, to-day a mighty host of Conservatives and Liberals; whilst on his left, scattered on two benches, a meagre dozen Labour Peers.

Finally, we would go to Buckingham Palace, and wait outside the gates until our gracious Majesty drives out for an airing. "Now," I would say to my guest, "you have seen with your own eyes all the three parts, King, Lords, and Commons, which together make up the British Parliament."

"But," I should add, "please understand that everything that you have seen, all the persons, together with all the Members of Parliament who were absent, and the Prince of Wales and his brothers, and even the picturesque royal palace of Westminster and the stately Buckingham Palace, together with all the Government Departments, might be engulfed in an earthquake never to reappear, without destroying, or even weakening, the social institution which we call the British Parliament." The very next day another King would be proclaimed, within a month a new set of Peers and Members of the House of Commons would be assembled, a new Civil Service would be appointed, carrying on exactly the same forms and ceremonies and with precisely the same constitution and activities as before. In fact, a social institution is not a tangible thing at all; it is simply a relation between persons not attached to any one of them, but transmitted, by an invisible force, from group to group and generation to generation.

Can we say that a social institution exists and exists only in the minds of men? This would be going too far. Relationships between men are as much part of the external world as the men themselves; as individual events they can be observed and recorded, described and measured. If observation and reasoning be correct, the way in which these relationships will work in the future can be foreseen. It is only in its entirety or wholeness that a social institution eludes direct apprehension and finds its embodiment in an idea.

Professor Hogben has suggested to me that a social institution is like a species. A species of plant or animal cannot be observed in its entirety; we cannot see all the dogs or all the men in the world; we can only observe some individuals, some specimens of the species. But unlike a species, a social institution is indestructible by any force external to the mind of man. At the same time it may seem the most fragile form of life, because it exists only so long as people think or feel about it.

Supposing you could, by some miracle, extirpate all the emotions and all the thoughts and memories about the King, Lords, and Commons from the minds of everyone concerned, the British Parliament would disappear. And as human beings are inherently co-operating animals, some new thought about human relationships would spring up in the minds of men or of the predominant men, and become embodied in a new form of social organization. Indeed, we do not need a miracle to be aware of this process. In our own lifetime, after the Great War, we saw the Emperors and their Court officials, together with their Councils of State, of three such mighty races as Germans, Austrians, and Russians disappear in a few days, even in a few hours, to be succeeded in the twinkling of an eye by other social organizations, temporary or permanent.

A study of social institutions, of their birth, their growth, their decline and their death, consists therefore of innumerable studies of the behaviour of individual men and women when these individuals form themselves in particular groupings or in particular relations to each other and to the rest of the community. We discover this behaviour and these relations by direct and indirect methods. If we desire to study the past of social institutions we examine the vestiges of this behaviour in fossils and ancient monuments, or we study the records of human activities in documents and contemporary literature. When we investigate existing social institutions, we add to this evidence of past events what we can learn from other people and what we ourselves observe of the behaviour of particular individuals on various occasions and in particular circumstances. And finally, when we want to get some proportionate view of this behaviour of individuals, we use the statistical method, we count and we calculate, so as to ascertain how many persons act in one way and how many in another; in other words, we measure the action and reaction of man as a social being in this or that environment.

But whatever methods we employ, what we are always observing and reasoning about is not the working of a single organism; it is the behaviour of countless individuals, when grouped together in this or that relationship; as man and wife; parent and child; warriors and priests; masters and slaves; members of a profession or competing traders; as consumers or producers, to mention only one or two of the innumerable groupings which make up social institutions past and present.

Now the first step in the study of social institutions

—as it is the first step in the study of plants and animals—is some sort of classification, so as to concentrate our attention on one or other aspect of our subject-matter. I have found it useful in the study of social organization to divide up social institutions, past and present, according to the way in which they have arisen.

Thus I group social institutions into four types arising from or moulded by (1) animal instinct, (2) religious emotion, (3) abstract principles about the right behaviour of man which I will term humanism, and (4) deliberate planning, whether empirical or scientific, of particular forms of social organization in order to attain specific ends, for which class I shall use the term "technical."

The first species of relationships, the predominant one in all primitive social institutions, is derived from the animal world, more especially from the vertebrates. I say deliberately the vertebrates—that is, all animals with back-bones—in order to exclude the ants and bees, who stand at the head of another line of animal development.

Mr. Leonard Woolf suggested, indeed asserted, that the behaviour of human beings, as manifested in certain modern social institutions, might, and in fact did, develop into something approximate to the behaviour of the individuals in a beehive or in a colony of ants. Now we sometimes speak of a particular word as a "term of abuse": I call this analogy an "analogy of abuse", for he uses it as a warning

against social institutions he happens to dislike. I
note, by the way, that this contemptuous reference
to ants and bees was used by Dean Inge, Sir Hilton
Young, and Dr. Ernest Barker, in order to condemn
or deride social institutions they disapproved of.
Being men of exceptional talent, they loathe the
prospect of such a predetermined and regular life
as that of the beehive and the ant-hill. But they
need have no such fear.

Human beings are so made that they will always
be the very opposite of ants and bees. So far as I
understand the teaching of biology, this reference to
ants and bees is beside the mark. Men and insects
belong in fact to two experiments that nature seems
to have made in opposite directions. The behaviour
of the ant or the bee is part of its inheritance; and
just because it is so automatic, it no more demands
thought than does our movement away from the
motor-car which threatens our destruction. Your ant
or bee is born adapted.

On the other hand we trace in the back-boned
animals the gradual supersession of inflexible instinct
by a new and more effective kind of mental organization. Many vertebrates, other than man, habitually
employ the method of trial and error. They play,
they tease, they fight, they defend each other,
adapting their tactics to circumstances; they fear
the unknown; they have the imitative faculty and
even show inventiveness. It may be suggested that
in this inventiveness they are transcending instinct

and are beginning to have intelligence and, unlike the ants and bees, are becoming self-conscious.

When we come to man, even primitive man, we find that he starts off with comparatively few instincts; adapting himself, as he grows up, by learning what to do. The whole development of man, and therefore of his institutions, is one long replacing of mere animal instinct by feelings and thoughts. The most complete supersession of the automatic responses characteristic of ants and bees arises in that complicated mental process of observation, reasoning, and verification, which we know as the scientific method. Hence there is no sort of analogy between the complications of the beehive and ant-hill on the one hand and, on the other, the type of social behaviour repugnant to Mr. Leonard Woolf, expressed in social institutions deliberately planned to attain certain specific ends, such as the Scientific Management of American Capitalism or the General Plan of Soviet Russia.

Now as I am neither a biologist nor an anthropologist I am not going to betray my ignorance by assuming that this or that human institution can be detected in the social behaviour of some lower animals. How well I remember the guide, philosopher, and friend of my childhood—Herbert Spencer— telling me delightful tales about the social behaviour of beavers and penguins, of monkeys and apes; proving conclusively that they not only evolved the institution of the family, monogamous, polygamous, matriarchal and patriarchal, but also leadership, organized hunting and fighting, with its delight in mastering, killing, and even torturing other animals; mob panic, professional theft; play and sport; property rights and territorial jurisdiction; the search after and hoarding of food, and even the collection and transporting of equipment for the home, individual or collective. To-day I gather that notable biologists dismiss much of this prehuman social behaviour as "travellers' tales"; they assert that the only social institution common to man and to sub-human animals is the family. "The cause which gives rise to the formation of a group among animals, and the bond which holds such an animal group together," we are told by Briffault, "are in every instance manifestations of the reproductive instincts, and every association of individuals in the animal kingdom is, without exception, a reproductive organization." I cannot tell you whether this Freudian view of the social behaviour of animals is or is not correct. Zuckermann in his recently published book on *The Social Life of Monkeys and Apes* gives us a dividing line between the sub-human and human social behaviour. "The effective stimuli involved in the behaviour of animals are mainly inherent in immediate physical events, which are in no way the by-products of the activities of pre-existing animals of the same species. Man, on the other hand, amasses experience through speech, and the effective stimuli underlying human behaviour are largely products of the lives of pre-existing people."

I am inclined to think that the dividing line between man and the rest of the animals is to be found in the use of speech. I may add that the animal behaviour, typical of primitive social institutions, may be and often is subconsiously present in the relationships set up by social institutions ostensibly derived from religious emotion, humanistic theory, or applied science. For even if all behaviour be at root animal, it is worked up into different patterns according to the presence in the human beings concerned of religious emotion, humanistic theory or the capacity for applied science, or any combination of these three faculties of the human brain.

I pass to my second class: social institutions arising out of, and dominated by, religious emotion.

Early in the evolution of human society, so we are told by the anthropologists, man began to reflect on the nature of things; whether he saw these things awake or in his dreams, he inferred a principle of life, like that of which he was himself conscious, and which we are now accustomed to call a soul. "Millions of spiritual creatures walk the earth unseen, both when we wake and when we sleep" the poet tells us. Towards these spirits, primitive man experienced the emotion of fear, leading to all sorts of magic and to the medicine man, afterwards to become the king by divine right. Then there arose the emotion of wonder and adoration, leading to worship, of love leading to prayer and the merging of self in the spirit of love; from whence arose devoted service in carrying out what tradition or holy writ, sometimes interpreted by the prophet or priests, declared to be the will of God. All this culminated in the great religions of historic time, Judaism and Christianity, Buddhism and Islam.

Perhaps the dominant feature, and, I suggest, the survival value, of religious institutions, has been the curbing, some would say the canalization or sublimation, of man's animal instincts. The vows of poverty and chastity, the habit of fasting, all characteristic of religious orders, whether Christian or Buddhist, certainly directly contradict the animal appetites of human beings. We find always a code of personal conduct, it may be mere ritual, assumed to be spiritually inspired, and sanctioned by rewards and punishments, either in this life or in another. These religious institutions dominate the whole life of India; whilst the Ten Commandments of Judaism furnish the pattern of behaviour through the civilized world.

It is, I think, these codes of conduct that constitute the survival value of religious institutions. Perhaps the outstanding religious institution to-day is the Roman Catholic Church: ubiquitous and unchanging; autonomous within its own spiritual sphere; a state within a state; equipped with the most elaborate specialized technique; infallibility at the top, offering complete mental security; together with the celibate priesthood, strictly disciplined and habitually poor, and therefore disinterested in mundane affairs, continuously employing an empirical psycho-analysis in the periodical confession and absolution of all the faithful.

From social institutions originating in religious emotion there is a short step to my third class: social institutions arising out of our intellectual dogmas about the right behaviour and right groupings of man in society.

The characteristic feature of this class of social institutions is that the founders almost always confuse what *is* with what, in their opinion, ought to be. Hence I have termed this class "humanistic." The most famous of these political creeds is that embodied in the American Declaration of Independence, 1776. "We hold these truths to be self-evident: that all men are created equal; that they are endowed by their Creator with inalienable rights; that among these rights are life, liberty, and the pursuit of happiness; that to secure these rights, governments are instituted among men, deriving their just powers from the consent of the governed; that, whenever any form of government becomes destructive of these ends, it is the right of the people to alter or abolish it, and to institute a new government, laying its foundation on such principles, and organizing its powers in such form as to them shall seem most likely to effect their safety and happiness."

When we remember that, at the time of this

Declaration, and for nearly a century afterwards, negro slavery was the economic basis of a large proportion of the production of the U.S.A., the statement that all men are created equal with equal rights to life, liberty, and the pursuit of happiness, appears the most ironic fiction in the world's history. Whether the United States of to-day with its tiny minority of multi-millionaires, on the one hand, and on the other its millions of workless destitute persons, is consistent with an equal right to life, liberty, and the pursuit of happiness, I will leave to the American citizen to decide. In a slightly different form the same metaphysical idea of the rights of man is elaborated in the Declaration by the French National Assembly in 1789.

But, however divorced from reality this dogma of the inalienable rights of man may appear to-day, it did result in what seems to most of us a great step forward in human progress—namely, the establishment of political democracy in the U.S.A. and France, and the spread of this type of government to other countries during the nineteenth century.

A typical and no less amazing example of the overwhelming potency of an intellectual dogma is the course of events in Soviet Russia during the past decade. Here we see a stupendous refashioning of the social institutions of one-twelfth of the human race, spread over one-sixth part of the habitable globe, carried out according to the dogma of a German Jew of genius, Karl Marx.

I have not room to discuss the validity of the dogma of the materialist interpretation of history (the hypothesis being that political institutions are determined by economic conditions—such as the way a man earns his livelihood); nor can I discuss why this so-called law should lead to the supercession of the Dictatorship of the Capitalist by the Dictatorship of the Proletariat. But the use of the phrase Dictatorship of the Proletariat—which clearly, if it means anything at all, means government by the whole mass of manual workers—to describe the rule of a highly intellectualized, strictly disciplined, and rigidly exclusive Communist Party will, I think, be regarded by future historians as a fiction no less audacious than that of the American dogma that all men are born free and equal, with equal rights to life, liberty, and the pursuit of happiness. All the same, the purpose of the Soviet experiment, which many of us expect will ultimately prove successful, is the establishment, for the first time in history, of a network of social institutions amounting to an equalitarian state, in which all men have equal chances of life, liberty, and the pursuit of happiness.

My fourth class of social institutions is on a different plane from any of the three classes that I have described. In these types of organization it is the desired end, whether the satisfaction of animal appetites, the fulfilment of religious emotion, or the carrying-out of the humanistic creed which is the decisive mark.

When we come to the most modern of social institutions we find that they are of the nature of devices or expedients consciously and deliberately adopted for the purpose of carrying out, with greater efficiency, previously determined ends or ideals. Thus the purpose of the institution falls into the background. It is the perfection of the means of machinery used upon which the mind of man is concentrated. Efficiency, efficiency, and again efficiency becomes the be-all and end-all of human effort. The special feature of all social institutions of this type—which I call the technical or scientific— is that, whatever the desired end or purpose, the specific institution is deliberately planned and put in operation according to the methods of applied science.

In my examples of social devices thus arrived at, I confine myself to new and modest institutions which may not even have occurred to many of my listeners as institutions at all. How many of you have thought of the audit of public accounts, or the introduction of Summer Time as social institutions? They were certainly not derived from animal instinct, or from any religious emotion, or even from any conception of the inalienable rights of man. They are based on observation of the behaviour of men in particular circumstances, with the object of altering that behaviour so that it should correspond to some actual or imagined public convenience. And because they are so contrived they have wrought in the lives of men changes positively greater in magnitude than some of the most ancient of customs or the most authoritative of creeds.

To this category belong not only what the American capitalists call Scientific Management, and the Five-Year Plan of Soviet Russia, but also the codes and services in every civilized country, of public health and public education, of factory regulation and the handling of traffic on our crowded highways, of the organization of military forces for offence and defence as well as innumerable arrangements for the improvement of our machinery of government.

All these forms of social organizations are put in operation to achieve an end or to fulfil a purpose which has been defined for them—perhaps by what I call animal instinct, perhaps by religious emotion, perhaps by humanistic dogma, or perhaps by some empirical notion of public service or public safety. They are consistent with any scale of values in human society or with any conception of the relation of man to the universe. Here, as elsewhere, science is concerned with the processes of life and not with the purpose of life: science can tell you how to kill or how to cure a man, but it cannot tell you whether you want or should want to cure or kill a man; that depends on the emotional side of your nature: cynics would say on subconscious self-interest or capricious taste; idealists would say on your religious or humanistic faith.

And here I should like to point out that it is

exactly because science deals with means and not with ends, with process and not with purpose, that we need not fear the advent of an inevitably uniform "Scientific Society" throughout the world. Whether the continuous preoccupation of the most enlightened men and women with the perfecting of the technique of social institutions—whether the specialization be that of an orchestra or a scientific laboratory; the machinery of government of a great nation or a chain of multiple stores; the organization of an army or navy, or that of an international system of television—will, in practice, lead to indifference to the purpose of human life—to the absence of any agreed scale of values, and to the gradual disintegration of all codes of conduct, private or public, I do not know. If it does it will land us in social chaos.

2. THE DRAWBACKS OF DEMOCRACY

I HAVE not space to discuss the imperfections and the shortcomings, or what we may call the diseases, of all the different social institutions. I cannot even examine specimens of all four classes. I must confine myself to two outstanding social institutions of our own time, political democracy and the capitalist system.

I define political democracy as the government of the people according to the voices or votes of the people. This means in practice, government according to the will of the majority of voters. It is only at a Quaker's meeting that no decision is arrived at, and no action taken, until there is agreement among all the members. This procedure would be clearly impossible for the purposes of political government.

The question immediately arises, Who are "the people"? Does this term imply the inclusion of every adult inhabitant of the country concerned? If so, political democracy is the growth of the last thirty years. For the so-called democracy of ancient times, and even the democracy of the United States, established in 1776, excluded a large class of slaves. And if we are to consider women as persons, and not as chattels, women were everywhere excluded, until the latter part of the nineteenth century, when New Zealand, South Australia, and two states in America gave votes to women.

The first obstacle in the way of the application of democracy to government—and one which is very apparent in Eastern Europe to-day—is represented by the presence of determined minorities of race, religion, or language, having their own peculiar traditions or habits, living in the midst of majority communities, with quite other needs, loyalties, and aspirations. To such minorities a democratically elected Government, working through majority rule, may seem as tyrannous as an autocratic monarch. The fact that Irishmen were represented at Westminster even more fully than Englishmen did not stop the movement for Irish Home Rule. It was this hatred of alien rule, and not any desire for the happiness of the common people, that led to the setting-up of the self-governing cantons of Switzerland, and to the establishment, as independent democracies, of Greece and Italy. This dread problem of minorities leads to chronic disorder and all too often to civil war. One way out is the surgeon's knife of separation: for instance, the breaking away, quite peacefully, of Norway from Sweden. Another way is to parcel out the functions of government so as to allow each obstinate minority to govern itself in such matters as language, education, religious organization, the laws regulating family life, and, indeed, every other social grouping, in which the minority has needs and ideals contradictory to those of the majority.

What is the secret of the strangely seductive charm

of this particular form of government? For political democracy has spread within a couple of centuries from country to country, alike in Europe and all over the American continent, north and south. It has captured the imagination of the multitudinous races of China and India, whose ancient civilizations excluded the very idea of it: it has even attracted the adoring gaze of Africa's primitive tribes.

I suggest that the magic of political democracy lies in its enlargement of human personality. The newly enfranchised human being, whether white or yellow, brown or black, whether male or female, feels that he has grown in moral and intellectual stature—he has lost a sense of inferiority—he has gained new interests, new responsibilities, new powers of making the world more as he wishes it to be. Oddly enough, as every experienced administrator knows, this enlargement of personality actually increases his docility, or at any rate makes him more easy to govern. This is due to the consciousness of consent in which, I suggest, lies the "survival value" of political democracy. In a democracy the laws are obeyed, just because the people, with or without reason, believe that they have consented to them.

But the consciousness of consent must be not only to the project, but also to the performance. It matters little whether the electors voted for the project or not; the crucial question is, Will they like it when they have got it? As you all know, the people of the United States voted, by an overwhelming majority, for the prohibition of alcoholic drinks. But when prohibition was put in force, large sections of the population, among them many of the wealthiest, and most influential, disliked it, and disliked it so intensely that they brought into existence whole organizations of smugglers, illicit stills, and boot-leggers, developing into racketeers, blackmailers, and murderers, all in an illegal conspiracy to defeat the objectionable law. This lawlessness, especially on the part of the rich and the powerful, is perhaps the most fatal of all diseases of democracy; because it is apt to become an epidemic, and to spread down-wards, from the few who are rich to the many who are poor. Such a widespread withdrawal of consent to the existing social order leads to the loss of the survival value of political democracy, and therefore, to its probable supersession by one or other form of dictatorship.

Let us consider how this loss of the conscious-ness of consent occurs, and what are the remedies for it. The first thing we notice about the electors in a great modern constituency is their lack of interest in, and knowledge of, about nine-tenths of the work of government. And this does not apply only to the less educated classes. The university don, the great business magnate, the busy lawyer or medical man, is as ignorant of some departments of public admini-stration as the mechanic or labourer is of others. The public-spirited and intelligent factory hand and miner will know a lot about factory legislation and mines regulation Acts—about the provision of elementary schools—of public-health clinics—of the sanitation of the mean streets—of the presence or absence of open spaces, public libraries, baths and wash-houses, or pollution of the air and water in mining villages or the poorer quarters of great towns. The medical man may be conversant with the Public Health Acts; the banker may understand currency and credit; the merchant may have some sort of opinion as to the relative economic advantages of free trade and protection. But the sphere of knowledge and sympathy of each individual is usually strictly limited. We rarely find in any section a clear understanding of that part of the government which specially affects, for good or evil, the lives of the other classes.

This is, of course, an overwhelmingly strong argument in favour of admitting all the inhabitants of a great country as equal voters. But it does very little to counteract the will-lessness characteristic of a great democratic population when it goes to the polls. For we have to remember that the all-inclusiveness of political democracy implies the presence on the register of persons, rich and poor, who have no public interest whatsoever. They either abstain from voting or are driven to the poll by mob fear or mob greed. "Hang the Kaiser and make the Germans pay" is the sort of programme that appeals to them. How terribly we have all paid and are still paying for the consequences of this slogan on the Peace of Versailles, Sir Arthur Salter has told us. So far as I have observed British electorates, and read about the electorates in other countries, I see no evidence of any general will common to all vocations and all classes: the idea that there is a general will inherent in any community of human beings is a myth, and a mischievous myth at that.

This absence of any general will on the part of the electorate has led to the rise of political parties; groupings of men and women holding strong opinions of how the country should be governed and by whom it should be governed. The express purpose of this party organization, nicknamed by the Americans the "caucus," is to create among the electors a general will in favour of particular men and particular measures—a particular group of persons as representatives, and particular measures to be carried out by Parliament and the Cabinet. We trace the first beginnings of widespread party organizations to the United States which had, owing to universal male suffrage, constituencies of hundreds of thousands when England had electorates of hundreds.

As might have been expected, the caucus that began in Great Britain was definitely connected with the extension of the suffrage to the working class in the last quarter of the nineteenth century. Pray do not imagine that party organization in our own country did not exist in previous generations. For a hundred years it had been embodied in the groupings of the great Whig and Tory families. With the advent to power of the industrial middle class after 1832, it became incorporated in two exclusive social clubs—the Carlton and the Reform. What was resented about the caucus of the 'seventies and 'eighties was not the existence of party organization; it was the inclusion of working-class members, in the main the work of Joseph Chamberlain. How proud he was of his famous Six Hundred of Birmingham, mostly working men! This social institution of a caucus spread rapidly all over the Midlands and the North Country; consequently Chamberlain was denounced not only by the Conservative Party, but also by the right wing of the Liberal Party, for inaugurating something approaching to a Dictatorship of the Proletariat— a monstrous danger to the State, so it was held.

Now it is well to realize that in a political democracy we cannot do without organized political parties. If we are to secure the consciousness of consent from a multitude of electors, made up of rich and poor and practising all sorts of trades and professions, there must be groupings of men and women having a common political faith, led by men who will undertake to carry out this party programme, should they come back victorious from the polls. Without such alternative programmes and such alternative groups of men, ready to carry out a given policy, the electors would have no intelligible choice and would be powerless to influence the action

of the assembly they elected. But the formulation
of a policy involves propaganda. Thus we watch
political parties seeking to create what has been
found to be absolutely necessary for the work of
government, a common will among the inhabitants
in favour of this or that policy in home or foreign
affairs. And this propaganda affords, incidentally, a
method of educating the electorate to understand the
work of government. It is essential that this party
programme should be based on some sincerely held
opinion as to public welfare, whether that opinion
takes the form of maintaining the present state of
affairs or of altering social organization, in one
direction or another, in order to obtain a higher
civilization.

But we must remember that this party organization, like all other social institutions, is liable to be
perverted, to become diseased. Whilst professing to
promote the welfare of the people, a political party
may, in fact, work for corrupt ends; that is, for the
promotion of the private interests of individuals or
corporations. In the United States both the Republican and the Democratic parties would appear to
be intent, not so much on fulfilling their openly
professed programme of rival ways of social better-
ment, as on obtaining power, for the purpose of
giving their friends remunerative posts and giving
the corporations who have supported them valuable
contracts or grants of land or oil or water privileges.

But the same insincerity and duplicity of behaviour

may take less invidious forms. The party organization, if it comes to represent not a genuine philosophy of social welfare but only the pecuniary interests of a particular class, may carry out when in office a legislative and administrative policy which its most enlightened members know to be injurious to other classes. Each party may, in fact, pander to the demagogues of its own class against its better judgment. Some would say that the drastic cutting down of beneficent social services on the one hand, in order to avoid taxing the rich, and on the other, the reckless giving of unconditional outdoor relief, irrespective of its affect on character, in order to increase the incomes of the poor, are symptoms in our own country of the disease of demagogy in party organization, against which every wise citizen ought to struggle.

To my mind a political party ought to be a sort of church—a Congregation of the Faithful, with a definite code of conduct, whether private or public conduct, and a clear vision of what sort of behaviour they wish to bring about in the community as a whole.

What a political party ought *not* to be is a business corporation, intent on the pecuniary self-interest of its members as individuals, or even of any particular section of society, represented in its membership.

But faith alone will not suffice. There must be knowledge, if ideals are to be realized.

Sometimes when I lie awake at night and consider

what I would do if I were a millionaire, I end up with a plan for endowing every political party, of a specified magnitude, with the means of maintaining an adequate research department, of its own appointment, charged with the discovery and classification of every kind of fact bearing upon the party's projects and programmes. The more I hated the policy of the party, the more anxious I should be to provide it with a research department. For knowledge of how things happen in society cures a multitude of prejudices and unwitting cruelties, while it opens the way for agreement among those with common ideals, but advocating different means of reaching those ideals.

But I should make my handsome subsidy on two conditions. First, each research department should forthwith communicate all the facts that it discovered or collected to the research departments of the other political parties, just as the several secret services attached to our principal Government departments immediately pass on to each other everything that they severally discover. My second condition would be that, prior to publication, all statements of facts should be submitted to a High Court of Auditors, aided by scientific assessors in all branches of political and economic science, and representing all political parties. Such a court would pass judgment on these facts as naked facts, unclothed with any inferences or arguments; and confer upon those adjudged to be true the high privilege of a National Mark. Any facts not so admitted could, of course, be published, but would be published without the National Mark. By the way, this public audit might be applied to statements of fact appearing in newspapers, if these were challenged by a certain number of readers; the newspaper being under the statutory obligation to print the report by the Board of National Audit.

An equally disastrous, but I am glad to think a more easily remedied disease of democracy, is the perpetual decay of the political constitution regarded simply as part of the machinery of government. Somehow or other, in Great Britain and the United States, and I fancy in some other political democracies, the existing constitution, whatever it may be, is regarded almost as sacred—as something which cannot be changed without a violent upheaval. How comic this seems in a changing world! Is it not plain that the machinery of government necessarily requires the same incessant overhauling and repairing in order to adapt it to the new facts, as the machinery of a power station or the organization of the railways?

In Great Britain we suffer terribly from this outworn machinery of government. One of the oldest and certainly one of the ablest of our elder statesmen, Mr. Lloyd George, told us in 1931 that the House of Commons is "like an old windjammer which was equal to the traffic of a hundred years ago, but cannot cope with one-hundredth part of the enormous trade of to-day." The six hundred members find themselves, not with too much to do, but with nothing what ever to do that seems worth doing. This feeling of frustration on the part of the representative is handed on to the constituency. The unfortunate member finds himself perpetually explaining and excusing his powerlessness to influence either legislation or administration.

And now what about the permanent Civil Service? —for after all, as Mr. Leonard Woolf has already remarked, it is they who carry on the work of government. The Civil Service, like the electorate and like a party organization, suffers from dangerous diseases which may damage or destroy its value to the commonwealth. There is the disease of favouritism and nepotism. There is the still worse disease of what is called in the u.s.a. the "spoils" system. This means that, on a change of government, all officials are dismissed, in order to replace them by partisans of the new administration. This can be prevented by giving security of tenure during good behaviour.

Of course, there are some who think that the mere existence of a salaried Civil Service is a disease— they call it "bureaucracy." Frankly, I cannot understand what is meant by this objection to salaried Civil Servants as such. Usually it comes to no more than a suspicion that there are far too many Civil Servants. I can only say that my own experience is that every Government department in the country is —to the detriment of the public service—greatly understaffed, and far from excessively paid, if we are to accept as a criterion the earnings of similar

N

brainworkers in profit-making industry. I am afraid that what is meant by most of those who complain of bureaucracy is that they object altogether to the work of Government, and would like to see much of this superseded by profit-making private enterprise.

However this may be, it is significant that private enterprise to-day has created an enormous bureaucracy of its own. A multitude of salaried persons is, in fact, merely one of the necessities of enterprises on a large scale, whether profit-making or governmental.

Assuming that I am right in my contention that the principal defect in political democracy is the will-lessness of the electorate, what are we going to do about it?

First, we must recognize that each person is under an obligation to remedy the defect in himself or herself. Secondly, I suggest that those who have not yet made up their minds should not wait until the next General Election, but should start straight away to find their own political souls. Why not write to the headquarters in London of the three political parties—Conservative, Liberal, and Labour—asking them each for a statement of their principles and programmes? Then study these pamphlets carefully, and decide which one is nearest your own view of the right behaviour of man in society. Then go to the nearest public library, or, if there is none near you, to the most intelligent Conservative, Liberal, or Labour man you happen to know, and ask him for the title of a book on any part of the programme that specially interests you. Read this and any other literature you can get hold of.

When you are sure which party you prefer, ask to be admitted as a member of its local organization and help to convert other people to its programme. Then you, at any rate, will have played your part in remedying the will-lessness of the electorate, with its inevitable symptoms of lack of faith and lack of knowledge—a will-lessness which is the most deadly of the diseases afflicting political democracy.

3. THE CAPITALIST SYSTEM

As the term is sometimes misunderstood or mis-applied, I will begin by a definition of what I mean by "the capitalist system."

I mean the particular stage in the development of industry in which the bulk of the workers (in the Britain of to-day, about four-fifths of the whole population) find themselves driven to work at wages for the owners of the instruments of production whether land or capital. This type of industrial organization came gradually into existence in Europe and the United States within the last few centuries, dating, shall we say, from the fading away of feudalism at the close of the Middle Ages. It has latterly spread, to a greater or lesser degree, all over the world.

This does not mean that there were not men of wealth, and even great financial magnates, before profit-making capitalism. I need not remind you of the ancient slave-owner who owned the workers as well as the instruments of production. The social institution of slavery underlay the civilizations of Egypt, Greece, and Rome, not to mention the primitive institutions of many savage races. In the Middle Ages there was not only the king and the great feudal lords, who owned the land and exercised authority over serfs and freemen; there were also the money lenders who lent money at interest to kings and nobles, merchant gildsmen, master craftsmen, and peasant cultivators alike.

The characteristic feature of the capitalist system, which began to dominate British industry in the eighteenth century, was the fact that the peasant cultivators, domestic manufacturers, master craftsmen, copyholders, and other types of individual producers, who had hitherto themselves owned the instruments of production, and sold their product for their own advantage, gradually changed to the position of mere wage-earners, working under the orders of the new industrial capitalists owning machines and using power. These workers came to be called, not men and women, but merely "hands." The new employers could easily dispense with the legal ownership of their employees, for they held in their hand the whip of starvation. There came to be few alternative ways of earning a living. If the workers failed to obey the mill-owner's orders they were dismissed to something near starvation. Thus the Capitalist system as it existed in Great Britain in the eighteenth century and for the first quarter of the nineteenth, whether in the mines or in the factories, on the fields or on the ocean, implied control over the worker's life not only during working hours, but also in the home and very largely also in the way in which he spent his earnings and his leisure time.

Now it is not my business here to pronounce judgment on the Capitalist system, or to sum up its advantages and disadvantages in comparison with any other social institution. Like Political Democracy, Profit-making Capitalism has outstanding advantages, otherwise it would not have spread from country to country. I think it has been proved that the capitalist system of industry was a great advance, measured in human happiness, over the slavery characteristic of ancient civilization or the hierarchy of privileged classes dominating the mass of the population in the Middle Ages.

In his great book, *The Wealth of Nations*, Adam Smith described how the old order of Corporations and Trade Guilds, with its exclusion of illegal—that is, unapprenticed—men, and its maintenance of ancient processes of manufacture, fixed rates of wages and customary prices, prevented the most enterprising and energetic manufacturers and merchants from making fortunes. This making of individual fortunes seemed to Adam Smith the one and only way to increase the wealth of the nation. Though each capitalist rightly thought only of his own profit, yet this motive of pecuniary self-interest actually steered them, Adam Smith said, "as if by an invisible hand" to promote the prosperity of their fellow-countrymen. Accordingly, it became the fixed opinion of the whole capitalist class that any interference with their freedom, whether by law or by custom or even by religion, was not only foolish but also downright wicked.

For more than a hundred years the achievements

of the capitalist system surpassed everybody's expectation. All sorts of machines were invented, to be driven by wind, by water, or by steam, so as to manufacture fifty times as much as could be done by the skill of the handicraftsman. Roads and canals and railways quickened and cheapened the distribution of the ever enlarging mass of goods. Ships of larger size, presently driven by steam engines, carried coal and the commodities produced from cotton, flax, wool, silk, or iron, to all the countries of the world. This industrial development was made possible only by the accumulation of large fortunes in the hands of the employers. Meanwhile the continuous expansion of industry created innumerable salaried positions, and provided certain sections of the manual working wage-earners with money incomes greater than most of them had previously enjoyed.

If Adam Smith could have lived to know the capitalist system as it existed in Great Britain in the middle of the nineteenth century he would have felt that his analysis of 1776 had been fully borne out by the facts. Regarded as a social institution for the creation and accumulation of wealth in Great Britain, capitalist profit-making had been supremely successful. How far this century of success had been due to the exploitation of other countries, in which the growth of capitalism had been delayed, may be a matter for discussion. What concerns me here is not the rise and progress of profit-making Capitalism;

but the liability of this particular social institution to perversion or disease, and the steps that have been taken, or that may hereafter be taken, to prevent or counteract these evil tendencies.

It was only gradually realized, in the course of the nineteenth century, that there was another side to the picture. Amid all the wealth and national prosperity, there was also being created a mass of human misery. In pursuit of profit, by the increase in output and the lessening of cost, some of the capitalist employers stuck at nothing within the law. In many cases the factory operatives were required to work for intolerably long hours, without rest-pauses or holidays. They were subjected at the factory and in the mine, as in the over-crowded hovels in which they had to live, to insanitary conditions and the risk of avoidable accidents involving sudden death or maiming for life. The harnessing to the machine of the woman and the child proved seriously detrimental to health, broke up family life, and brutalized the town population. In the slums of the manufacturing towns what modern industrialism was destroying was the soul of the people.

For there is a moral miasma as deadly as the physical. Right down to our own day the dwellers in the poor quarters of the great cities of Europe and America, actually in increasing numbers as one generation follows another, find themselves embedded, whether they will it or not, in all the ugliness, the dirt, and the disorder of the mean streets.

Breathing, from infancy up, the atmosphere of the slums, subject to long periods of unemployment, with insufficient food and with no means of healthful recreation, the average man is, mentally as well as physically, poisoned.

Can we, from an examination of the effects of unrestrained capitalism during the early part of the nineteenth century, diagnose the disease from which the social institution itself suffered?

The harm done was not intended; it was not a case of personal cruelty. It was sheer callousness to the state of things which the capitalist system had created. The capitalist was often a man of great intelligence and good will, an excellent father and husband and colleague. His callousness was what is called in modern scientific jargon merely a conditioned reflex from his environment. Living in a material environment of ease and plenty, of power and freedom, and continuously occupied with the technical problems of his quite reputable vocation of profit-making, he simply had not the time or the energy or the opportunity to study and reflect on the lives of the workers. He lived and had his being in a sphere of thought, feeling, and action, which was wholly divorced from the conditions of the workers. And this state of mind became more and more dominant, when the capitalist was not himself the manager of his works, but merely the chairman of a joint stock company; or a financier who was providing the capital; or one of a multitude of shareholders who did not know even where the works were, and never came in contact with the workers.

Callousness was, in fact, an inevitable disease of modern capitalist production. I speak from personal experience. Both my grandfathers rose, in the eighteenth century, out of the class of domestic manufacturers and master craftsmen, leaving most of their relatives to be transformed into mere wage-earners. One a Liverpool merchant, the other a Manchester warehouseman, they were men of exceptional energy and of great public spirit. My father inherited the vocation of profit making. He became a promoter and manager of railways, a chairman of an English railway and a President of an American railway. He and his colleagues were undoubtedly good men. Yet in the mental and social environment in which they were born and bred there was no kind of thought or feeling about the condition of the wage-earners.

Labour was, to those engaged in big business, a natural force, like electricity or water; it had to be manipulated, in order that work might be performed and private profit made. "Water plentiful and labour docile" was a phrase I remember in the prospectus of one of my father's companies. If the labour was no longer needed it was left, like waste water, to sink into the ground. It was taken for granted that the poverty of the poor was the inevitable result, if not of Divine Providence, at any rate of a natural law. "Without a large proportion of poverty," exclaimed Patrick Calquhoun, the inventor of the modern police system and a contemporary authority on the resources of the British Empire, "there could be no riches in any country, since riches are the offspring of labour, while labour can result only from a state of poverty. Poverty is that state and condition of society where the individual has no surplus labour in store, or, in other words, no property or means of subsistence but what is derived from the constant exercise of industry in the various occupations of life. Poverty is therefore a most necessary and indispensable ingredient in society, without which nations and communities could not exist in a state of civilization." And this moral callousness was reinforced by the metaphysic of orthodox political economy, and by even the actual experience of profit-making enterprise. How could you give higher wages or shorter hours, better sanitation or greater comforts than those usually prevalent? How could you avoid using poisonous substances or dangerous processes, if your competitors behaved in that way? The pressure of competition by other manufacturers made it imperative, under pain of ruin, to seek every possible reduction in working costs, even if this meant chronic disease or continuous underfeeding for men, women, and children.

Now, fortunately for the capitalist system of industry and for the community in which it flourished, it was eventually discovered that the worst effects of this disease of callousness could be, if not wholly prevented, at least largely mitigated. This was done by the growth of two other social institutions—The Trade Union Movement and Political Democracy.

Here is an interesting point. It is one of the peculiarities of the pathology of social institutions, as distinct from the pathology of individual organisms, that there is often a remedy to be found for the evil incidentally caused by one social institution in the setting up of another social institution. Thus we can cure the bad behaviour of an autocratic monarch by establishing some sort of Parliament to keep him in check. We can remedy the administrative incompetence of a body of representatives by creating a permanent Civil Service. Thus we watch in Great Britain during the nineteenth century the rise of the Trade Union Movement with its device of the Common Rule and its two instruments for its enforcement, collective bargaining, and legal enactment. We see, on the other hand, the development of Political Democracy in social services. By the influence of these two newer social institutions, the community has, step by step, so surrounded the Capitalist System, whether by Trade Union regulations or by Factory Acts, or by such public sanitation, public education, and provision for the casualties of industry, that the callousness characteristic of the capitalist system has been progressively checked and counteracted.

I wish I had time to deal with the Trade Union Movement, which has its own drawbacks and diseases—very serious drawbacks and diseases. All the same, trade unionism, in my opinion, has raised the standard of life of the worker, and, what is equally important, enlarged his personal freedom and increased his personal dignity and self-respect.

But trade unionism was not the only social institution counteracting the disease of callousness in the profit-making employer. There are the social services of public health and public education; of health and unemployment insurance; old age and widows' pensions; and, last but not least, municipal housing; in fact, all that we know as state and municipal socialism. Unfortunately, we are threatened to-day with a set-back alike in trade unionism and in the social services. Mass unemployment has destroyed the bargaining power of trade unionism, whilst the cry of economy has starved the social services. We are told that owing to the world-wide shrinkage of markets, profit-making industry can no longer provide the nation with an income sufficient to afford these beneficent activities.

And here I come to the most fatal of the diseases to which profit-making capitalism is subject; and one that neither trade unionism nor the social services have, so far, been able to prevent or to cure.

Has it occurred to you that capitalism suffers from planlessness? Each grower of wheat or producer of rubber, each manufacturer of clothing or books, each ironmaster or coal-owner, insists on expanding or contracting his production according to his individual judgment of how he can make the largest profit, without any common estimate of what the world actually needs. Indeed, the invariable feature of the planlessness that characterizes competitive capitalism, whatever else it produces, it does create and perpetuate the sovereign evil of unemployment in one country or another, and increasingly throughout the whole industrial world.

Nor is this disease of planlessness, which seems to beset all competitive capitalism, confined to countries of partial development, or having inadequate resources, or lacking industrial organization, or overburdened with war debts. Just the same booms and slumps, just the same alternations of chronic overtime and mass unemployment, just the same perversion of profit-making in such anti-social activities as adulteration, noxious drugs, company frauds, and stock exchange speculation and swindling exist in the United States as in Great Britain; in the European countries of the highest technological development, as in those, such as Australia and South America, in which conditions are still relatively simple. Is this absence of any deliberate planning inherent in the independent pursuit of profit by individual capitalists?

It is no answer to this diagnosis to say that, when the capitalist produces too much or too little, or produces what the world does not want or cannot pay for, he makes losses instead of profits, and may even be ruined. Whenever the capitalist makes a mistake, the world suffers, and especially the wage-earners, who find themselves unemployed. Moreover, when one set of capitalists makes a mistake, not only the community suffers, and the wage-earners who lose their employment, but actually also most of the other capitalists throughout the world, who find that the unemployed wage-earners can no longer purchase the commodities that have been quite properly produced for their consumption.

This planlessness, as it seems to me, is the gravest and most intractable disease from which the social institution of profit-making enterprise is now suffering, not in one country only, but all over the world. It is the fundamental cause of there being to-day at least twenty million workers, through no fault of their own, unemployed in the dozen countries in which capitalism has its most perfect development; representing a quarter of the whole population of the United States and of Europe, excluding Russia. And if my diagnosis is at all correct, there seems nothing that Capitalism itself can do to cure the disease of planlessness from which the social institution as well as all the world is now suffering.

In the series of talks on "The Changing World," broadcast in the autumn of 1931, this disease of planlessness was constantly recurring as the main cause of the economic blizzard bringing disaster to the whole business world. Some speakers emphasized this planlessness in connection with the supply of credit; others with the maldistribution of the gold of the world. Others attributed to the same planlessness both the frenzied speculation on the New York Stock Exchange in the autumn of 1929, and the panic-stricken hoarding, in safes and stockings, of hundreds of millions of pound or dollar notes throughout the U.S.A. and Europe in 1931. Another school of economists recognized a similar planlessness in the enormously increased output per worker, due to ·the reckless adoption of new mechanical inventions by capitalist enterprise throughout the world, irrespective of the consumers' purchasing power—a purchasing power automatically diminished by every displacement of wage labour, and the consequent spread of mass-unemployment.

J. A. Hobson tells us in an article in the *Manchester Guardian*, on the "World Crisis," that the failure of profit-making capitalism is due to the fact that it ignores any provision for consumption. "The new capitalism," he tells us, "can only prosper by restraining the new powers of productivity it brings into being—surely a monstrous paradox." In the December number of the *Monthly Review* issued by Lloyds Bank, we are warned that "the world is rapidly drifting into a situation where all would be sellers and none buyers; and this is but a synonym for commercial deadlock and breakdown."

"Our impoverishment is in the midst of plenty," said Sir Arthur Salter, "Indeed," he adds, "it is apparently due to over-plenty. Nature was never so prodigal with her resources. Man was never so skilled in exploiting them. What does this mean? It means, can only mean, that the intermediate system that stands between producer and consumer and that adjusts supply to demand, especially the monetary and credit system, has broken down."

In a most fascinating study of American Capitalism Dr. Bonn, the eminent German economist, writes: "If the depression lasts sufficiently long, it will not be simply a case of criticism of this or that measure, or this or that individual. It will not be merely a question of subsidies and of relief work. The crisis of economic policy may very easily become a crisis of the economic system. . . . The real significance of the American crisis," Dr. Bonn sums up, "consists in the fact that to-day it is not merely the present American economic leadership or economic policy that is being questioned, but the capitalist system itself."

"Our Socialists say that Capitalism is on trial," observes Mr. Arthur Chamberlain in his chairman's address to the Tube Investments Ltd., Birmingham, "If this, indeed, be so and it fails to win its case, it will be not because it could not, but because it would not; because, in fact, it presented such a poor case that people said 'nothing can be worse than this, let us try State management'—which is exactly what happened in Russia. The issue is in your hands. If you continue to accept failure with complacency while it is hatching, and hysteria when it is hatched, you will get all you deserve."

Let us examine the remedies proposed by accomplished statesmen and economic thinkers for the terrible disease of planlessness.

These remedies seem to run in two diverging directions. President Hoover and his "big business" advisers insist on what he calls the "American way" of leaving the great profit-making corporations free to concert together to devise some scheme by which, consistently with their own profit, they can bring back prosperity to that great continent. Meanwhile the nine or ten million workmen unemployed— equal, with their families, to nearly one third of the whole population—are to be left to the tender mercies of the philanthropic rich, so far as the Federal Government is concerned.

Sir Arthur Salter, on the other hand, points out that whilst a general plan carried out by the capitalists of the world could have prevented the present terrible disease of unemployment, yet the capitalists seem to have been unable to come to any such decision. "The knowledge was available, but the knowledge was not utilized; the power was not concentrated; the action was not concerted." Sir Arthur Salter goes on to suggest that the State should compel the capitalist profit-maker to concert with his fellows, and produce a plan for so organizing production and distribution as to provide regularly what the consumers need, and so employ continuously those same consumers as wage-earners. If the social institution of capitalism cannot be so transformed, Sir Arthur Salter suggests, then the State must step in more drastically, so as to "combine safeguards to the public interest, with scope for private initiative." He cites as examples the B.B.C., the Electricity Commissioners, and the proposed London Traffic Board. "Public supervision needs to be proportionate to public interests," he gives us as his axiom. Thus, wherever public interests are concerned, the planning should be by governmental or semi-governmental authority, which means that the acquisitive instinct of profit-making enterprise should be replaced by the motive of public service; that, in fact, private enterprise should be superseded by public administration.

I do not presume to offer an opinion where such great experts and authorities differ. Nor do I think it is possible to-day to arrive at any common agreement about the relative advantages of profit-making enterprises and public administration. For it so happens that two great nations, on opposite sides of the world, each comprising over a hundred million people, each having almost unlimited resources, each virtually protected by its magnitude against foreign intervention—are "trying out" the relative efficacy of an almost unbridled Capitalism on the one hand, and, on the other, an almost complete State Socialism.

The relative success of American Capitalism and

Russian Communism in yielding a good life for the whole population; whether this be measured by material prosperity or by the development of human personality, will, I think, largely influence, I might almost say determine, the social and industrial organizations in Great Britain and throughout the civilized world.

Dean Inge, in his brilliant vision of himself as a world Dictator, emphatically endorsed the "American Way" as a "marvellous achievement full of encouragement"; whilst he condemned, dogmatically and without qualification, the social institutions of Russian Communism.

I am content to wait and see.

PROFESSOR W. G. S. ADAMS

II. HAS PARLIAMENTARY GOVERNMENT FAILED?

1. MACHINERY OF PARLIAMENTARY GOVERNMENT

IF we are to answer this question—Has Parliamentary Government failed?—we must clear our minds as to what the question means. It may mean different things. First, it may mean that parliamentary government has failed and should be replaced by some alternative system. If we take this view we must be prepared to show what the alternative is.

Or second, the question may mean only that Parliament does not work as well as it should; that it has failed to do many things which it should do and has done other things which it should not do. This does not mean that an alternative system to Parliament is required. It is simply that the personnel and policy are not what they should be.

Or there is a third meaning to the question. We may think that the system is defective, but that it has to be reformed rather than abolished; that new machinery is required to supplement the work of Parliament but that we can build upon the foundations which Parliament offers.

Now if we hold the first view, that the parliamentary system should give place to some other system, we must be prepared to state what is the alternative. Parliamentary government is one form of representative government and there is, of course, the alternative to representative government itself, namely, direct government. Direct government means that the people themselves propose and vote laws and elect officers to carry them out. But such a system of government can only be applied in very small communities or to a very limited extent in large national communities. So we must look for an alternative amongst the forms of representative government. Now the nineteenth century saw a very considerable extension of representative government in Europe, but this was in the direction of parliamentary government, or of a form of government which is first cousin to parliamentary government—the American system of congressional government. It was left to the twentieth century to develop distinctively new types of government, such as the Fascist Corporative State or the Russian Soviet system. These types of government are also representative, but they differ in fundamental principles from the parliamentary or congressional type. They are based on the domination of a single party and they involve restrictions on the rights of free speech, of free association, and even of free movement. The State is under the strict discipline and direction of one party which does not permit any challenge to its authority.

We may doubt how far systems which rest upon the restriction of such fundamental rights afford an alternative way of government to countries which set a high value on these rights.

Looking, therefore, to parliamentary government rather than to any alternative, let us consider briefly two questions. First, What is the nature of the parliamentary system in this country? Second, what distinguishes some other types of parliamentary government? In England we speak of the sovereignty of Parliament, by which we mean the King in Parliament—the King, Lords, and Commons. But under the parliamentary system the powers of the King are exercised by his ministers. The royal veto in legislation has ceased; the veto of the House of Lords has become mainly power to delay. The House of Lords to-day serves the function of advising and warning the House of Commons and the nation, rather than of being able to decide for them. Power has thus been more and more concentrated in the House of Commons. Meanwhile the House of Commons has been made much more widely representative. Just one hundred years ago the first Reform Act was passed, which opened wider the door into Parliament. By successive steps the door has been opened further, until now it is wide open and, broadly speaking, all adults, other than criminals and lunatics, have the right and duty to record a vote. But the distinguishing characteristic of the parliamentary system is not only that the people elect representatives, but that they choose the Government. Ministers sit in Parliament and are responsible to it. They cannot continue to hold office unless they have the confidence of the House of Commons. Thus the parliamentary system gives us responsible government.

Now the underlying principle of this way of government is that there is freedom of choice and equal opportunity for all parties to be represented. The will of the majority rules. The only right of the minority, it has been said, is to persuade the majority, and the minority must have full and free opportunity of doing so. There are therefore in all true forms of parliamentary government, not one but two or more parties. Constitutionally there is an Opposition, as well as a Government. And in time the Government becomes the Opposition and the Opposition becomes the Government.

We have said that the King has ceased to exercise the veto, and that the responsibility for his acts rests with his ministers. But circumstances do still arise when the King has to use his discretion in inviting a political leader to form a Government, and you cannot entirely eliminate such discretion. The incoming minister takes responsibility for the King's decision, and Parliament gives or withholds its confidence. There is in this way complete constitutional parliamentary control. The Executive is thus fully responsible to the Legislature. But it is not entirely subordinate to it. A great characteristic of our constitution is its balance; there is a fine sense of balance in the relations between the Legislature and the Executive. For behind the sovereignty of Parliament lies the sovereignty of the people; and the custom has grown up whereby when the Government is defeated on a vote of confidence the normal procedure is that the King should grant ministers a dissolution of the House of Commons so that the people may decide in what Government they will place their confidence. This use of the prerogative to grant a dissolution of the House of Commons has not only kept Parliament in closer touch with the people but at the same time has strengthened the power of ministers and maintained the balance between the Legislature and the Executive.

Again, concentration of power is an essential of good parliamentary government, and this concentration of power has in the English constitution been most clearly developed by the growth of ministerial responsibility. In no country has this principle been so deeply rooted in the working constitution. It is often said that the English constitution, and its parliamentary system, is not based on logic but on experience. It is based on experience, but the deepest logic is that of experience. The sovereignty of Parliament and ministerial responsibility are great logical principles which bind together the whole structure of government. Ministerial responsibility is a key principle of our parliamentary system.

Let us take an example of how this principle has been developed.

British constitutional liberty has centred largely round the question of financial control. The House of Commons has been jealous for centuries of its financial privileges. But the House of Commons has also been quick to see the importance of financial responsibility, and so more than two centuries ago it laid down in its Standing Orders that no proposal for taxation or expenditure could be made except by a minister of the Crown. By giving ministers this great power we have been able to develop a system of control over taxation and expenditure the importance of which has not always been realized by other countries which have adopted a parliamentary government. Hence, also, the great caution which the House of Commons has shown in its development of committees on finance. Committees may review and report, but they must not be allowed to weaken the sense of ministerial responsibility for finance. Here there must be no divided control. So again, the House during the nineteenth century has given more and more to the Government the control of the time of the House of Commons, and has left to ministers the work of initiating most of the important measures of legislative policy. This is due mainly to the fact that to an increasing extent modern legislation of a constructive social and economic character involves public expenditure. And all such measures must be Government measures. Thus it is that there has been a steady concentration of power not simply in the Commons, but in the Cabinet, whose most important ministers sit in the Commons.

Let me mention only one other characteristic of our constitution which flows from the sovereignty of Parliament—the flexibility of the constitution. The constitution can adjust itself continually to new conditions. It is capable of expansion in many directions and of absorbing into itself new forms of government, of permitting decentralization and recentralization of functions as circumstances require. These are at least some of the outstanding features of the parliamentary system as we know it in England.

Let us consider how certain other like systems differ from ours. We may for comparison look to three countries—France, Switzerland, and the United States of America.

The parliamentary system of France offers the most instructive comparison with that of England, partly because it is modelled to a considerable extent on the English system. The present form of parliamentary government in France has now stood for sixty years. It consists of a system of two chambers: the Chamber of Deputies, elected by adult male suffrage, the Senate, chosen by a system of indirect election. The Government depends, though to a less extent than in England, on the support of the lower House; but there is one important difference. Whereas in England the normal procedure when the Government is defeated on a question of confidence is to dissolve Parliament and appeal to the people, in France, when a ministry is defeated it gives place to another ministry without any appeal to the people. In France, Cabinets change, but the Chamber remains, and because of this there is not that same degree of contact between the Chamber and the people as there is in England, nor is there that assurance that a crisis can be solved by a declaration of the will of the people. In France ministries are short-lived and unstable as compared with England. On the other hand, there has grown up in the French Parliament a remarkable development of committees which provide, in their own way, an element of stability and continuity. In the Chamber of Deputies these committees are in most cases appointed for the whole statutory period of the Chamber's life, namely, four years. They are representative proportionately of the different parties, and in that sense they mirror the life of the Chamber, and they concern themselves with legislation, with finance, and with policy. The result is that in practice the committees weaken the power and the responsibility of ministers but give to the individual members of Parliament a greater share in the shaping of policy and in the criticism of administration.

Switzerland offers a great contrast to France. For whereas the government of France is highly centralized, Switzerland has a federal constitution which has been built up out of the local governments of the cantons, and in no country has the citizen been able to take a more direct part in the work of government. Switzerland is one of the great political laboratories of the world, and is famous above all for the part which direct government has played in association with a system of parliamentary government. The *referendum*, by which the people are called upon to give their approval to constitutional changes and to certain other important measures, and the *initiative*, by which the people can propose legislation, have been devices of popular government which an increasing number of other countries have adopted. Especially if one regards the post-war constitutions of Europe, the influence of the Swiss experiments in direct government can be seen. But a great French constitutional writer has said that Switzerland is to be admired rather than imitated; and we must be careful about applying the experiences of a country with the traditions of Switzerland to one with a very different background. Even in Switzerland, despite its great traditions of direct government, the ordinary work of legislation and administration is entrusted to the representative assemblies, and to their executive officers.

This brings me to note a second distinctive and characteristic feature of Swiss democratic government. In Switzerland, the Cabinet is made up of members of different parties. Ministers are regarded as the servants of the Legislature, and if their policy is not accepted they do not resign; they simply bow to the will of the Legislature and carry out its policy. This results in a permanent non-party executive. So that the State has in charge of its affairs political leaders of long and continuous experience. And this has given Switzerland a very stable administration and what has been called a business type of government. It is a model very well worth careful consideration in certain conditions, but we can hardly regard it as a substitute for the English Cabinet system. Nevertheless, Switzerland, politically, socially and economically, deserves careful study. There, at least, the most democratic forms of direct and parliamentary government do not lead to revolutionary changes, but are on the whole conservatively progressive. Switzerland also has given the world a great lesson of how, under a free constitutional system, peoples of different race and creed and even language can live together and how local freedom can be reconciled with national unity.

If we turn to our third example of popular government, that of the United States, we find a system which has been called Presidential or Congressional. The outstanding contrast between the constitution of the United States and that of England, France, or Switzerland is the great extent to which in America, the Legislature, the Executive, and the Judiciary are independent the one of the other.

The President is chosen by the people, and the President, in turn, chooses the Cabinet, and neither the President nor his ministers may sit in Congress. Congress consists of two chambers, the House of Representatives and the Senate, elected directly by the people. The President is largely independent of Congress and Congress is largely independent of the President. The one is a check upon the other, and their agreement is necessary towards an effective constructive policy. This separation of powers has contributed to the rigidity of the American constitution, which can be changed only by a three-fourths majority of the people. In that respect America is less democratic than Switzerland, or France, or England.

But despite these differences the American system resembles in many ways parliamentary government. The President and Congress, though independent, must work together in legislation, in foreign policy, in finance, and even in administration. Party is a great link in bridging the separation of powers, and the United States has maintained the two-party system. On the whole the American and English constitutions seem to be coming nearer one to the other. But England has a more flexible type of government and can adjust itself more easily than the American constitution to changing conditions.

It is necessary to comment on another notable type of recent institution, namely, the modern German parliamentary system. This is a very interesting form of government which has borrowed largely from the experience of other countries. Germany, however, has not simply borrowed from other constitutions, she has also created a new instrument of representation. Alongside of the two Chambers of Parliament, there has been set up an economic Parliament called the Imperial Economic Council, which has important powers of initiative and advice, but its legislative proposals have to be passed like other measures by the two houses of Parliament. Even if the German Economic Council has not achieved as great a success as it was hoped, it is by far the most important experiment which has been carried out in the effort to combine in a parliamentary system a special chamber dealing with economic and social questions alongside of the old territorial system of representation. Anyone who is trying to answer the question, "Has Parliamentary Government Failed?" must watch the future of the German constitution.

Everywhere parliamentary systems are learning by experience how they can be improved, and we are yet far from seeing the perfect type. So that when we are judging the system we must think, not simply of what it is but of what it can be. This is a matter of the very greatest importance to us. England is the country which has given the world parliamentary government. All things considered, England still offers the best model of parliamentary government. But we have to see that we do not rest on past achievements, or be content with a system which worked well yesterday but may be unequal to the tasks of to-day and to-morrow. We have to test and examine our working system, consider its defects, see how it can be improved, and boldly create where the conditions call for boldness.

In this way only can England continue to uphold the reputation of parliamentary government. We must not forget the great heritage of political liberty which has been worked out through this instrument. The last people who should doubt parliamentary government or decry its qualities are the people of this country. Can we show in these times that here is an instrument capable of taking into itself new elements of control, new methods of representation, new means of initiative, and of proving that it still is a system flexible, resilient, equal to the task of carrying out whatever policy may be the will of the people?

2. DEFECTS OF PARLIAMENTARY GOVERNMENT

MOST human things, however good they are, have the defects of their qualities. Parliamentary government is no exception. It has its defects and its dangers, and if we are to make parliamentary government as good as it may be we must be on the watch for its shortcomings and think how we can remedy them. We shall find that many of our small defects can be traced to one or other of three greater matters: first the defects of the party system; second divided responsibility; and third congestion of business in Parliament.

Before we proceed to examine these matters let us remind ourselves that the parliamentary system is based upon freedom of discussion, the rule of the majority, and the right of the minority to persuade the majority. And let us remember that Parliament itself has two great functions. First, it has to frame laws and to shape policy; second, it has to provide the ways and means of carrying out its policy and of controlling its administration.

Moreover, the end of parliamentary government is not representation—it is action. Representation is a means to the end of finding out the will of the people and of enabling that will to be put into effect. If, for example, our system of representation is so complicated, or leads to so many divisions amongst us that there is no clear will of the majority in Parliament, then Parliament is apt to become little more than a talking-shop, and parliamentary government loses the confidence of the people. John Stuart Mill said in his *Representative Government* that the business of Parliament was "bavardage," "talking." Speaking of legislative assemblies, he said, "*talking* and discussion are their proper business, while *doing*, as the result of discussion, is the task not of a miscellaneous body but of individuals specially trained to it." It is essential to our parliamentary system that there should be full and free opportunity of discussion. It is the very breath of its life. But discussion must lead to action.

Let us first consider defects in connection with the party system.

Party is in itself a good thing. The parliamentary system requires parties if it is to work. It naturally breeds parties. But parties, if they are to be healthy, must represent principles. The party system, as we know it, is liable to defects and we have to think how it can be kept healthy. As I have said, one of the things which distinguishes parliamentary government from the Soviet and the Fascist systems is that the latter have only room for one party. They are one-party systems, and in them public discussion is directed to working out what the principles of the party are supposed to permit. But this idea, while it may be necessary for certain States in passing through a period of crisis or revolution, is not compatible with parliamentary government. Wherever there is freedom of opinion there are bound to be different parties. But there are dangers which we must note.

The first danger is a multiplicity of parties or groups which leads to such division that there is no clear majority. This has been a weakness in many of the parliamentary systems in Europe from which both France and Germany have suffered. The people have at times been divided up into so many groups or parties that it is difficult to ascertain the will of the majority or to maintain a stable combination of groups; and for that reason the two-party system, where the two parties do represent principles, is the best working system. It places issues more clearly before the people. It makes responsibility much more definite. It works in with our Cabinet system of collective responsibility—for the two-party system not only helps the Cabinet system, but the Cabinet system tends to keep in existence the two-party system. Of course there may be more than two parties in a good working parliamentary system. There may be on important issues more than two alternative views; then rightly there will be more than two parties. Where the party system breaks up into a number of groups or divisions, there the working of parliamentary government will be more difficult and less satisfactory.

A very different kind of defect is that the party may become rigid and try to shut out independent opinion. This is a danger to which one-party systems like the Fascist or the Soviet are specially exposed. Parliamentary government is based on toleration. The party system sometimes becomes intolerant. The party machine is apt to become too dominating an influence and to regiment and discipline the voter or the member of Parliament. It is a danger to which the two-party system, as we see in the United States, is always exposed.

A third defect is that parties tend to treat everything as if it were a party matter, whereas in fact many things ought not so to be treated. One of the signs of progress in our parliamentary system is that, to a greater degree, we have come to consider certain subjects not as party matters. Thus in international and foreign affairs there has grown up a tradition of continuity and co-operation between parties. A change of Government may in some measure affect the way in which our foreign affairs are handled and the national attitude towards them; but on the whole parties do not try to make capital out of foreign affairs. Again, the same is true of Imperial affairs. From time to time questions arise which stir up party strife, but, speaking broadly, neither foreign affairs nor imperial affairs are now of a party character.

Take a third example: the more constitutional questions, such as how to improve our machinery of government, or the organization of Parliament itself, or the electoral system, can be kept out of the clutches of party, the better. After all, these are matters in which all parties have a common interest: they are the servants of all parties. A real advance was made in parliamentary organization in the nineteenth century when the Speakership of the House of Commons was taken out of party politics. After the first Reform Act, it was felt that the Speaker, though a member of Parliament, should not join in party controversies: he should be above party. This wholesome convention has now been observed for one hundred years, with the result that the Speaker if he is willing and able, has invariably been re-elected from Parliament to Parliament, no matter what Government was in power. In no parliamentary system in the world does the Speaker hold a position of such dignity and impartiality as in our House of Commons, a fact which has enabled the House to commit to the Speaker powers which could never be entrusted to a Speaker who was of a party character. Thus, under the Parliament Act, the Speaker has been given the very great power of deciding, with the advice of two assessors, whether a Bill is or is not a money Bill.

In the same way, if the procedure of the House of Commons, if our electoral system, I would even go further and say if the question of the House of Lords and its reconstruction can be kept outside party, there is a gain to the nation. And this is not something outside practical politics. In 1918 the two Houses of Parliament set up a joint conference consisting of members of all parties to consider the best way in which the Second Chamber might be reconstituted, and the result of that very important conference, under the Presidency of the late Lord Bryce, showed a great degree of agreement amongst its members. It is most desirable that we should think out the subjects which should be above party.

Let us now consider the second defect of parliamentary government—divided responsibility.

Democracy likes divided responsibility. The people must divide in order to rule. Sometimes the people distrust their representatives. They treat them as if they were delegates. Sometimes the representatives distrust ministers, and they have committees to keep ministers in check. In a good parliamentary system the people treat their members as representatives, not as delegates. "Your representative owes you not only his industry but his judgment," said Burke to his electors. In a good parliamentary system also the ministers have the trust and confidence of the Legislature. The strength of the one-party system and of the dictatorship of an individual or of a party is that there is not divided responsibility. There is unity of command.

One of the great organizing principles of our parliamentary system is ministerial responsibility, and we have attached importance not only to the doctrine of individual ministerial responsibility but to the doctrine of collective ministerial responsibility.

On the other hand, in France, where there is a highly developed committee organization in Parliament, divided responsibility becomes a serious menace to the efficiency of government. Committees divide authority with ministers, and the way in which on occasion the Budget is handled in France, and the extent to which the Budget Committee checks the minister and delays the Budget and divides responsibility, is a warning of the danger of divided responsibility. Again, where there are two chambers of Parliament with co-equal powers, there we see divided responsibility and the system does not work as well as where one chamber is responsible and the other chamber is given only powers of initiative, of advice and of delay. Our parliamentary experience has worked in this direction by concentrating power in the House of Commons and in the Cabinet.

But we may go too far in this direction. We may so concentrate power that we sacrifice liberty and even efficiency. Ministerial responsibility has its dangers. Our system of financial control has its defects. The power of the Government in finance may be so great that it practically prevents proper discussion and amendment of the proposals of the Government. Now genius consists in knowing where to draw the line. We have to secure a proper balance between the concentration of power and the opportunity for discussion and criticism, and when we consider the question of remedies, we must consider how the Committee system can be adjusted to the

Cabinet system without sacrificing the principle of ministerial responsibility. Order and liberty are both necessary to progress.

The third defect is the congestion of business in Parliament.

The sovereignty of Parliament gives us unity and order. But if this comes to mean that Parliament tries to keep everything in its own hands, then the system does not work properly and tends to break down. If we have not suffered as much as other countries from the defects of the party system or from divided responsibility, our Parliament has probably suffered and is suffering more than any other parliament in the world from congestion of business. Think of the things which come within the scope of Parliament. Everything from the private Bill of a local authority to the complex web of international affairs. It has to deal with the Empire, with the United Kingdom, and with the separate countries which make up that United Kingdom.

And the business of Parliament is not simply to make laws: it has also to look after the departments of public administration. In all modern countries there is a great increase in the work of the State— the number of laws has increased, the number of Departments of Administration has increased. Almost one hundred years ago there were complaints at Westminster that the business of Parliament was congested. Every few years after the first Reform Act we find members protesting that it is impossible for Parliament to get through its work efficiently. The number of measures which have had to be dropped at the end of a session for lack of time, the inadequate consideration of measures which are passed, the absence of effective discussion over policy and finance, these are reiterated complaints.

Our parliamentary system is highly centralized. Most of our self-governing Dominions, with a population very much smaller than the United Kingdom, have not only a central Parliament, but have local Parliaments. In Canada and Australia, there are the local Parliaments of the Provinces or States as well as the Dominion or Commonwealth Parliament.

The House of Commons has tried repeatedly to remedy this position by reforming its procedure. In the last fifty years it has introduced, in different forms, the closure as a means of regulating debate. It has developed a system of committees and has sought one way and another to prevent obstruction and to control the time of the House so as to get through its business. To some extent Parliament has been relieved by granting self-government to the Irish Free State, and by the setting up of a Parliament with powers to deal with domestic affairs in Northern Ireland. But until a more radical treatment is adopted than the reform of procedure can give the congestion will remain. It has made party discipline in the House, under the Whips, into something which depresses interest and initiative. The private member, during the nineteenth and twentieth centuries, has lost much of his freedom. The control of the time of the House has been concentrated to an undue extent in the hands of the Cabinet. Even so, the discussion of many measures is inadequate, and we have the spectacle each year of a large part of our national expenditure passing without any discussion. It is true that by devolving powers to its committees Parliament has obtained considerable relief, and that committee discussion is often much better than discussion by the whole House. But things have to come back from the committees to the whole House. You cannot remedy the situation by the best procedure in the world; you must go to the root of the trouble and pursue a bold policy of devolution—of decentralization.

Beside its influence on the working of Parliament there is also the effect which this congestion has upon the people. Democracy means that the people are associated as closely as possible with the work of government. Countries like England, Scotland, and Wales differ in their traditions and in their way of thinking in many important domestic matters. There are things which they should do in common, and that is what the Parliament of the United Kingdom stands for. But there are other things which they can do better for themselves. We have gone a considerable way in the direction of devolving administrative power during the past fifty years— since 1880. For example, separate departments for agriculture, for education, for local government, have been set up in Scotland and to a much less extent for Wales. But administrative devolution is not enough. Legislative devolution must follow administrative devolution. One of the functions of Parliament is to watch the administration and to ask questions about it, as well as to discuss legislation. Parliament has to see to it that the administration is working well, and if it is to do this, the Parliament of Westminster must shed part of its burden.

There is another aspect to this question of congestion. Parliament must also devolve special functions to special bodies, if we are to get the best results. The business of Parliament to-day is much more social and economic than political. Parliament is not an expert body on social and economic matters, and we must call to the service of the country those who have specialist experience in economic or social work. That is done by the German Economic Council. It has representatives of agriculture, of industry, and of the consumer, and its opinion is required on all projects of social and economic legislation and administration. We have taken some steps in that direction though different in character. We have set up in connection with our administrative departments like agriculture, education, trade, many advisory committees, and we now have in connection with the Cabinet the Economic Advisory Council.

I think there is much to be said for the way in which we are trying to solve this difficulty. But by some means or other, Parliament must devise machinery which enables the practical expert to assist the Government in organizing the social and economic life of the nation. Parliament, to a larger extent than it has done, may delegate powers of initiative to such bodies. It may look to them for criticism and advice in respect of rules and regulations which the administrative departments are called upon to make under many modern Acts of Parliament. Our parliamentary system has such great qualities that we need not despair of a system because of its defects. The sovereignty of Parliament and ministerial responsibility give us such strong principles of control, well tried out by experience, that we can dare to devolve without fearing the consequences.

3. REFORM OF PARLIAMENTARY GOVERNMENT

LET me draw attention to three ways in which we can look for an improvement in our parliamentary system.

The first, and by far the most important reform is to relieve the Parliament at Westminster of the domestic affairs of the different countries which make up the United Kingdom of Great Britain and Northern Ireland. Northern Ireland still remains part of the United Kingdom and sends its representatives to the Parliament of Westminster. But by the Acts of 1920 and 1922 there was set up in Belfast a Parliament for Northern Ireland to which was devolved from the Parliament of Westminster the responsibility for making laws and controlling the administration in such matters as agriculture, education, health, and local government.

I draw attention to this arrangement because it shows us an example of what devolution means. And there are eight years of working experience of this system to judge by. First we may say of it that in some measure it has relieved the congestion of business in the Parliament of Westminster. Second, Northern Ireland is now free to manage its own domestic affairs. The result is, to take one example, that there have been passed not one or two but a whole consecutive series of measures for the better organization of the agricultural industry in Northern Ireland. It is certain that it would have been a much longer time before such legislation could have got through the Parliament of Westminster. What is true of agriculture can, in different degrees, be said of other domestic matters. Northern Ireland can now build up its laws and its administration to suit its own conditions and needs. And if the laws are not good the blame lies with the people of Northern Ireland. That is what we should aim at doing for England, Scotland, and Wales: England needs Home Rule as well as Scotland and Wales. The Parliament of Westminster would then be relieved of a great deal of business and so be able to attend better to its proper concerns —foreign and imperial policy and the affairs of the United Kingdom as a whole. Moreover, the three countries in Great Britain would be free to manage their own affairs by their own laws and administration. The House of Commons recommended that the Government should do this as far back as June 4, 1919. The resolution which was carried on that date by a large majority is so important that it is worth quoting.

"That with a view to enabling the Imperial Parliament to devote more attention to the general interests of the United Kingdom, and, in collaboration with the other Governments of the Empire, to matters of common Imperial concern, this House is of opinion that the time has come for the creation of subordinate legislatures within the United Kingdom, and that to this end the Government, without prejudice to any proposals it may have to make with regard to Ireland, should forthwith appoint a Parliamentary body to consider and report:

"(1) Upon a measure of federal devolution applicable to England, Scotland, and Ireland, defined in its general outlines by existing differences in law and administration between the three countries;

"(2) Upon the extent to which these differences are applicable to Welsh conditions and requirements;

"(3) Upon the financial aspects and requirements of the measure."

In October 1919, in accordance with this resolution, a Conference was set up consisting of thirty-two members of Parliament, representative of both Houses and of all parties, under the Presidency of the then Speaker of the House of Commons, Mr. Lowther, now Lord Ullswater. This Conference held thirty-two sessions and reported to the Prime Minister its findings at the end of April 1920. It did not discuss whether devolution was or was not desirable. Its business was to consider the best ways and means of carrying out the resolution of the House of Commons in favour of subordinate legislatures within the United Kingdom. The Conference did not discuss a scheme of devolution for Ireland, though it came within its terms of reference, because it was known that the Government was actually taking steps to give effect to a scheme for Ireland. It dealt only with the three parts of Great Britain, England, Scotland, and Wales. Agreement, was reached on many important heads. First it was agreed that the units in which subordinate Legislatures should be established were England, Scotland, and Wales, and that the same powers should be granted to the Legislature of each of these countries. Second, there was agreement as to the powers which should be handed over by the Parliament of Westminster to the subordinate Parliaments. These powers were enumerated. All other powers not expressly enumerated were reserved to the United Kingdom Parliament. Third, the Conference was agreed as to the financial powers which were to be given to the subordinate Legislatures and also as to their powers regarding the judiciary. Thus there was very substantial agreement on many important points.

On the other hand, there was division of opinion as to how the subordinate Legislatures should be constituted. One half of the Conference favoured the proposal that the members of the House of Commons, for England, Scotland, and Wales respectively, should constitute a local "Council of Commons," in other words, that there should be no separate election for the subordinate Legislatures —and that there should be for each of these countries a small second chamber chosen by the Committee of Selection of the House of Lords. These two chambers together should form a Grand Council for England; similarly, there should be one for Scotland and one for Wales. These councils would exercise in their respective countries the legislative and financial powers devolved to them by Parliament. The scheme should be tried out for a period of five years, and during the two last years of that period the councils should be required to formulate proposals for the future of the scheme, either recommending a continuance of the Grand Council's system, or a return to the parliamentary system as it now is, or the establishment of separate Parliaments directly elected by the people of England, Scotland, and Wales, or such other scheme as might seem best.

The other half of the Conference considered that it was necessary from the first to set up subordinate Parliaments for England, Scotland, and Wales directly elected by the people, the personnel of these local Parliaments being thus distinct from that of the House of Commons or the House of Lords at Westminster. Some of the members of the Conference signified that they would be prepared to accept the first scheme, that is, using the members of the existing House of Commons to serve also in the Grand Council or local Parliament, believing that it would in all probability lead to the second scheme of directly elected Parliaments.

Whether as a result of this division of opinion or because Parliament was obsessed with other matters, nothing has been done. Half a loaf is better than no bread, and I would have taken the first scheme if I could not get the second. But in my opinion the right method is that of separate Legislatures for England, Scotland, and Wales. It effectively relieves the congestion of business in the House of Commons, and it allows the peoples of England, Scotland, and Wales, each to settle their own domestic policy. It is a quite big enough task for each Legislature. In our modern life the community sense is developing and nothing can foster this so well as a Legislature closely in touch with the people.

But in considering this question the size of the House of Commons, and still more of the House of Lords, should not be forgotten. We have in the present House of Commons 615 members. The United States of America, with a population nearly three times the size of Great Britain, has 435 members in its House of Representatives. The Commons, if substantially reduced in size, would be just as good a working chamber and the economy both of men and money would go some way towards meeting the needs of subordinate Legislatures. In the case of the House of Lords the present membership exceeds 700. The Senate of the United States, the most powerful second chamber in the world, is under 100. Therefore we should look to a very substantial reduction in the size of the House of Lords. On the other hand, the local Parliaments would sit in the countries which they represented. Men could serve in the local Parliament who could not give the time to attend at Westminster. The mistake should not be made of thinking that large Legislatures are desirable. Nor is it necessary that all these subordinate Parliaments should have second chambers. The more a Legislature deals with matters which affect the daily life of a people, the less there is the need of a second chamber.

But whether there is or is not a second chamber in such local Legislatures is of minor importance compared with the larger issue of an effective measure of devolution. I believe that this is by far the most important aspect of the reform of Parliament, and that if this reform is secured many other improvements will come with it. On the other hand, if devolution is not secured, all other improvements which can be made will be inadequate.

Let us turn to a second line of development which is sometimes regarded as an alternative to the setting up of subordinate national Legislatures. It is recognized that the issues which confront the modern State are largely economic and social; and it is suggested that what is required is that Parliament should set up an Economic Council or Parliament of Industry to which it should delegate its powers of legislation and administration in economic affairs. The German Economic Council is in a sense a chamber of the Legislature, and in Fascist Italy, where the community is divided up into great corporations, such as agriculture, industry, and transport, representation is largely of a group character. Personally, I do not think that the right line of advance in the British constitution lies in following such forms of legislature. But it seems to me that it is important that there should be effective representation of economic and social interests in connection with the administrative departments of the State. This is the direction in which we have been gradually and tentatively moving.

The beginning of this century saw the first notable step of this kind when in Ireland, under the Agricultural and Technical Instruction Act of 1899, there was established a representative Council in connection with the Irish Department of Agriculture. This Council and the Board elected by it proved the most admirable means of bringing the needs of the agricultural community to the attention of the Government. During the last thirty years there has been a growth of advisory or consultative committees, in connection with administrative departments, such as the Board of Trade, or the Ministry of Education. But something more than this is required. The great departments of State should have councils representative of the interests which they administer. The man who wears the shoe can tell where it pinches. The man who is engaged in agriculture or in industry or in health work or in education can tell whether the public department concerned with his work is fitting or failing. Such councils should initiate much of the legislation affecting our economic and social interests: legislation would then come before Parliament with great authority. Not that this is an alternative to devolution: it is a means of enabling Parliament to do its work of economic and social legislation more effectively. Yet in some degree it would relieve Parliament of the stress of business because measures would have already been discussed publicly in these special councils. The work of Parliament would then be to consider the effects of such proposals on the general well-being of the community and the financial obligations which they involve.

There is a third way in which experience indicates how our parliamentary system can be improved, namely, by the development of Committees. Other Legislatures have made much greater use of their members by means of Committees. One of the essentials of parliamentary life is that the members feel that they are sharing effectively in the work of Parliament. The principle of ministerial responsibility is fundamental in our parliamentary system: no development of the committee system would compensate for the loss of that responsibility. But the Committee system can be developed without weakening it. The function of a Committee is to examine, discuss, suggest; the function of a minister is to consider the advice of the Committee and to decide. So far from a right kind of Committee system weakening ministerial responsibility, it may be a paradox, but it is true to say that the power of a minister and of his department increases as they are in touch with public opinion. In recent years, after long effort, there has now been established a Committee on the Estimates which acquaints members intimately with the problems of the Estimates. Six hundred and fifteen members cannot possibly discuss measures satisfactorily: Parliament must delegate such work to an Estimates Committee; but it is also clear that the Estimates Committee must not detract from ministerial responsibility. Nor has the Committee done so. In the same way, in foreign affairs, surely there is an advantage in having a group of men representing different parties in intimate touch with the development of our policy, and providing a body of well-informed opinion on such subjects in Parliament and in the country? In the Legislatures of the United States and in France one of the most important Committees is that on Foreign Affairs. It is only by a considerable extension of the Committee system that the capacity of Parliament can be realized as a means of directing national policy and of educating public opinion.

And this brings me to a further point which should not be overlooked. It is of vital importance that the member should keep in close touch with his constituency. If we are to advance politically as a nation, it is not by the public choosing a member and then ceasing to take interest in the affairs of Parliament. Parliament should be a great centre from which public opinion can be enlightened and guided, but the Members of Parliament, if they are to do so, must bring back to their constituencies experience and information gained in Parliament.

In this way true democracy is made. It is only when we have a parliamentary system thus freed from serious and chronic congestion of business, assisted in its labours by the work of representative expert Councils, and invigorated in its membership by a good system of Committees, that the full value of our parliamentary system can be judged.

These are not new devices; they are the extension of methods which have already been tried in a limited way. Devolution has been at work for a period of years in Northern Ireland, but it cannot be seen to its full advantage unless it is part of a complete system. If there were devolution all round then the system in Northern Ireland itself would gain. But even with this limited devolution the advantages in relieving the Parliament of Westminster and in developing responsibility in Northern Ireland indicate what the system may mean if it were to be extended. Again, the use of special consultative councils has been steadily increasing. It is one of the ways of bringing local and central administration more into touch with one another, and it enables us, in a way which is more compatible with our parliamentary system, to do what Germany has been seeking to do through her Economic Council. We have already an Economic Advisory Council to the Cabinet. It often takes years before the full significance and value of such an institution is realized; only by trial and error can its proper place in the whole system of government be defined, but such a council may very well prove to be the crown of the Advisory Councils in connection with the various administrative departments. And then, slowly but steadily, the Committee system has been developing in the House of Commons: it has been a wise if cautious development, in which the principle of ministerial responsibility has been safeguarded.

Finally, there is the importance of developing closer relations between Parliament and the people. Parliament has already devolved on local authorities an increasing measure of public duties. Local Government is at the root of democracy. It is its great training-ground, and the more a sense of local responsibility and initiative can be developed, the more vigorous our national life will be. There have been tendencies in our system which were weakening local initiative and responsibility and increasing centralization. If the vigour of our local government is weakened, the whole of our political life is impaired. Parliament must continue in its work of devolving greater powers to local authorities. But with this growth of our local community life the importance of devolution to local Parliaments will become steadily more urgent. There is no solution to the problem in regarding the Parliament of Westminster on the one hand, and the Local Authorities on the other as adequate. International relations become more important; imperial relations are growing more necessary. It is vital that we have a central Parliament free to give its time wholly to these affairs. On the other hand education, public health, agriculture, local government, are also of vital concern to us as a nation. For these also we must have a body of men able to represent and guide public opinion. There is no other road for effective action than legislative as well as administrative devolution. If this is secured other things can be added; if this is not secured no other improvements can make good its loss.

If we believe that progress depends not only upon expert administration but that it requires freedom of speech and discussion, that it is based on toleration, and on the minority as well as the majority being able to voice its opinion, then there is no alternative to the parliamentary system in a democracy. Other forms of Government may for a time assert themselves, the domination of an individual or of a party may transform the organization of a State. But such systems are not truly democratic, and either they will continue to suppress a large part of public opinion or else they must develop the free discussion of divergent views which enables reason and conviction to remould policy in accordance with changing needs and changing opinion; they must move towards the parliamentary system.

There is no need to be pessimistic about our parliamentary system. The best definition I know of a pessimist and also of an optimist is that a pessimist is one who makes a difficulty of an opportunity, and an optimist is one who makes an opportunity of a difficulty. Of our difficulties we can make opportunities. Our parliamentary system has to be improved and developed to meet modern conditions. By such methods as I have tried to suggest, following the lines which experience has already taught us, we can build on the foundations already laid and show that the British constitution, if it is old, is also always renewing its youth. That is my answer to the question, "Has Parliamentary Government failed?"

PART III

WORLD GOVERNMENT

SIR ARTHUR SALTER

SIR ARTHUR SALTER

1. TRANSPORT AND TELEGRAMS TRANSFORM THE WORLD

GOVERNMENT needs to be constantly adapting itself to the activities it has to control or to help. It is always doing so; but it is always lagging behind. It is man's individual activities that set the pace. A new form of fraud occurs: and later a new law is made to stop it; a new abuse develops, and—later— a new regulation is made to restrict it. When the activities are confined within the area of a single country, and are but little affected by what happens outside, the task of adapting the methods of government is of course only a national one. The State may, for example, lay down new conditions for building houses without bothering itself what other countries are doing. But very many human activities have a range much wider than that of a single country. All industries, for example, which sell their goods abroad are affected by the laws and regulations not only of their own country but those of others. In such cases there is likely to be great loss and confusion if each Government acts separately without consultation with others. The question then becomes not merely of national, but of world, government.

If, then, we want to see how Government needs to adapt itself and its methods, we must start with some idea of the change in the activities with which it has to deal. We must see what men are doing before we can understand how to prevent them hurting their neighbours. Almost any change, anywhere, sets a new task for Government.

Let me illustrate by a single instance how the task of Government has become more complex. It is one of its first duties to prevent one man taking another's property. Under primitive conditions this might be physically difficult, but it was at least intellectually simple. A man stole a horse; he was caught; he was hanged. Contrast with this the intricate and abstruse issues involved when a modern company director is tried because of some words he has authorized in a prospectus. The law and its application need to take into account the complicated methods of financing modern industries, the standards of exactitude which have become customary in accountants' certificates and in the statements which are issued when new capital is raised. If the law did not so adapt itself, if it contented itself with punishing a man who stole physical and tangible property, it would obviously not be carrying out its first duty of protecting the citizen.

This is only one instance of the way in which, as the character of man's activities change, law, and the whole mechanism of government which creates and enforces it, must also change. There are, in particular, two spheres of human activity in which such changes in law and government, and especially world government, are needed. These are, first, economics and finance, and, secondly, political aspirations.

To understand, therefore, the problem of world government we shall have to consider the activities that have a world range. But before turning to particular subjects we must first deal with what is the main driving force behind all the changes that are taking place.

I shall first, therefore, discuss the way in which scientific inventions, and especially those which have improved transport and the transmission of news, have changed the life of man, and as a consequence have created an entirely new problem of world government.

The first thing we need to realize is the amazing pace at which the world has been transformed. Man has existed on the earth for many a millennium. We have recorded history of his progress and achievements for several thousands of years. But though, here and there, and for varying periods, he has established a high level of civilization and material comfort, there was till only about a hundred years ago one definite and unchanging limit to everything he did. He could neither move himself nor (with limited exceptions) send his communications faster than a horse could travel.

The difference which scientific invention has made in this respect in the last century is so fundamental that we must not only know it as a fact; we must use our imaginations to make all that it means real and living to ourselves. Let me try to help by a few examples. When Napoleon wanted to send a letter from Rome to Paris, it took him as long as it did Julius Caesar over eight hundred years before. The character of all his military plans and operations depended upon this fact; so did his relations with his Masters, the Directory, in the early part of his career. When Pitt sent instructions to his agent Wickham at Geneva he had to allow about a fortnight and wait a further fortnight for a reply. In 1834 when Sir Robert Peel was summoned back from Rome to be Prime Minister in a grave national situation, when speed was of the utmost importance, and he made every conceivable hurry, he had to lose twelve days on the way. It is the fact that a minister can now go to Geneva himself in eighteen hours by train, or six hours by air, or have a full discussion by telephone, without any loss of time at all, that makes a League of Nations materially possible as one hundred years ago a Holy Alliance was not possible.

Every method of government had, of course, to be adjusted to this limiting factor. The relative authority of every agent was dependent upon it. An ambassador, for example, who was separated by months from any instructions from his Government necessarily had a measure of independent authority that the telegraph and the cable were bound to destroy. And we still find queer bits of existing constitutions remaining, like fossils, from these earlier conditions. The reason, for instance, for the curious time intervals between the date of election and the date of office in the American Constitution is the long time which it used to take to travel from a distant State to Washington before the day of trains. You have a curiously uncomfortable time during which a Congress or a President holds office after its successors have already been appointed.

Transport and the communication of news, then, after being almost unchanging through all the previous ages of mankind, has been completely transformed in the space of less than two lifetimes. But the change once made, the pace of new invention has been stupendous. Within our own lifetimes, within even a single generation, there has perhaps been more scientific invention of such a kind as to change the very foundations of our life, than in all previous recorded history. And it is in the transmission of news that the change has been most striking and most far-reaching in its effects.

So rapid has been the succession of new inventions that we are only too ready to take each for granted as soon as the next one comes. If we are to stimulate our imaginations to the constructive tasks before us we shall do well to try to recapture the first thrill of the inventions of our day, to keep alive the sense of wonder and of the miraculous which we first felt. I well remember the thrill with which, as a young clerk in the Admiralty a quarter of a century ago, I first realized the new power of control given by wireless telegraphy. I had to arrange that a collier which had just left Gibraltar for Malta should return to Gibraltar to coal a warship. A week earlier I should have sent cabled orders to Malta and the collier would have taken a fortnight to reach them and then get to Gibraltar for her new job. But now I had the wireless; it caught her at sea and she was back in a couple of days. That, of course, is now the most commonplace of incidents—but for me it stirs the imagination because for me it recalls that first experience. I suggest that you should try to recall your own first experience of each new invention in the same way, before I ask you to follow with me some of the consequences.

Let me recount a personal experience, not my own, as a help to reviving this sense of the miraculous. It seems to me one of the most dramatic human experiences I have ever heard. It was told me a few years ago by an American who was a young aviator in the Great War. He was flying at night 2,000 feet above Washington. He had a wireless apparatus in his aeroplane to receive messages in Morse code. This was before the days of wireless telephony. He had never so much as heard of the possibility of speaking and hearing through the air. But, unknown to him, experiments in wireless telephony were being conducted. Suddenly he heard a voice speaking in his ear. His wireless apparatus had caught the first experimental waves of articulate sound. "I thought," he told me, "that my nerve had gone and my brain was turned. I came down as quickly as I could to find a doctor. I was instead directed to the experimenters to tell them of the success of their efforts." I can conceive no experience more weird than that of this young aviator, solitary, invisible, and blind, 2,000 feet up in the black heavens, with these ghostly and miraculous voices in his ear.

We must then think of the hurrying procession of train, steamship, motor-car, and aeroplane; of the telegraph, telephone, and wireless; the changes in man's activity and the organization of his life and work which they have brought. We must next in our imagination re-create the conditions of life before they came and contrast them with what we now see. And we shall then have some measure of the extent to which Government needs to adapt itself for its present task.

A hundred years ago mankind lived mostly in little and poor communities of village and market town, with a few capitals to which those not resident in them travelled slowly and rarely. The ordinary life of man, of making, selling, consuming, was, with few exceptions, within a narrow range. Not only each country, but each district, lived mainly to itself. It served its own wants, it depended for its fortunes mainly on its own efforts or the accidents of local events. Apart from war, the consequent increases in taxation, or rare pestilence, it was little affected by what happened a hundred miles away.

The craftsman would obtain his raw material of wool from the sheep in the fields around him, his power from the coal or water at his doors, and find his customers in his neighbours.

And so in a myriad economic units man lived his separate life. It was a poor life for it was limited to what could be provided by the skill and industry of a few people, aided by primitive tools and apparatus and utilizing resources available within a small area. Man had not harnessed nature to his service nor could he call upon the riches of different countries and the various aptitudes of many races. True there was some international trade. But it was mainly the exchange of a few staple products like woollen goods for precious metals or spices; a valuable addition— but a mere fringe upon man's normal life and work. Wealth and the standard of living were on a much lower level. But they were in some respects less precarious. Local disasters remained local in their effects.

Contrast with that the twentieth-century organization of the world. Sea transport from one hemisphere to another at a cost that may be an almost negligible item in the price of the article. A financial system which with amazing effectiveness and rapidity collects the savings of the French peasant or the farmer of the American Middle West and pours them in a fertilizing or wasteful stream into the Centre of Europe or Latin America. A system of money and distribution which enriches the table of typist and artisan with the fruits of every clime and continent. Above all a mechanism for the communication of news which, through the intricate network of finance, transmits in a moment the effects of whatever happens anywhere throughout the habitable world. The fortunes of the remotest factory or farm are at once injured by a shortage or misuse of gold; by excessive Government debts or foolish commercial policies; by others' reckless borrowing, or the alternation of optimism and pessimism of remote and distant investors. Our prosperity is greater but it is more precarious. Mr. H. G. Wells in his book on the *Work, Wealth and Happiness of Mankind* gives a vivid illustration of the dependence of all of us on conditions outside both our control and our knowledge. Indians starved in Labrador, he says, because a war in Europe changed the demand for furs.

Now this ease and rapidity of communication might of course be expected to correct and compensate for local disturbances and misfortunes; and so to bring a steadying element into the life of the world. So it should; and to some extent it does. If there are bad harvests in one continent there may be good ones in another. If one country needs capital for which its own savings are not enough it may utilize those of richer countries. This is true. But it is also true that when there are grave defects in the general system the range of the evil consequences is enormously increased. When a wave of folly seizes any considerable section of the world's population, the effects of their folly will be multiplied. And the very rapidity with which they act increases the feverish mood in which folly flourishes.

Now there is, unhappily, in our economic system—and has been ever since the Industrial Revolution—a grave weakness whose origin and character we do not yet fully understand, which causes alternations of prosperity and depression, of booms and slumps. The rapidity of modern communications increases both, and makes their effects penetrate more deeply into the life of every man in every quarter of the globe. The most striking instance is to be found in the speculative mania in America in 1929 and the crash which followed in the autumn of that year. It brought dislocation and disaster on a scale never previously known.

But we must never forget that this miraculous mechanism of rapid communications is at the service of wisdom as well as folly. It is at the service of those who are trying to regulate and control as well as those whose individual activities are creating new problems for government. I remember going into the office of the Governor of the Federal Reserve Bank of New York last June when the great financial crisis was imminent. The immediate point of danger was Austria. As I entered his room the Governor was turning alternately to a telephone on his right and on his left. He said as I came in, "The position in Vienna is grave. I am talking to Montagu Norman in London and the people in Chicago to see what can be done about it." So too, through the terrible crisis in the Far East, Mr. MacDonald and Sir John Simon have doubtless been able to speak to Mr. Stimson in Washington almost as if he were at the other side, not of a great ocean, but of the same table.

Science has given us a monster of illimitable power, to serve us or to destroy us. If we allow it, like a Frankenstein, to escape the control of our regulative wisdom, it will destroy us. But if we can keep control it can be the instrument of our salvation. The task of our age is to see that this Frankenstein remains our servant and does not become our master.

2. THE CLASH BETWEEN FRONTIERS AND TRADE

I NOW wish to look at this transformation in one particular sphere—that of world trade. Almost everything that a man does needs to be guided and restrained by law and administration to prevent it from injuring others. But laws are made and enforced by Governments; and Governments are national. When industry and trade therefore have a range that is wider than national sovereignties, they are subject to different, and it may be to conflicting, laws. Unless great loss and inconvenience are to be caused some agreement is necessary between the various law-making authorities. This creates a problem of world government.

If this were only a matter of making the same laws against theft and fraud, it would be a comparatively simple matter. But Governments are not content with this negative rôle. They use their power, principally by way of the imposition of customs duties, to give an advantage to selected national industries over their foreign competitors. It is this practice that causes the clash and conflict between world trade and national frontiers.

Let us pause and consider what an enormous difference this makes to the functions of government. The first task of government is usually to determine the conditions under which individual competition takes place; to maintain order and security, to prevent theft and fraud. It is like the task of a policeman keeping the ring clear, or an umpire insisting upon the equal observance of the rules by the competitors. Now imagine a world in which people were competing freely, except that Governments would stop them if they cheated. And then think of the difference it would make when all the different Governments began to help and hinder by putting up protective tariffs or giving bounties. It would be as if the policeman or the umpire suddenly jumped the ropes and gave a stimulant to one competitor and a blow to another.

It is evident that when a large number of Governments pursue this policy independently, with no common principles and without consultation, it is bound to cause the greatest loss and inconvenience to all those whose industries depend upon foreign sales. We should all agree, I expect, that they should at least try to arrange some common rules—so that, to continue our illustration, if Governments cease to be impartial umpires, they should at least, like the seconds at a duel, be subject to some code of behaviour.

I cannot, of course, now touch on the controversial side of tariff policy. Some people consider that a country loses by pursuing a liberal policy in a world which as a whole is highly protectionist; others hold the contrary view. I shall now express no opinion. But if we consider world policy as a whole, several things may be usefully said that are not contested or controversial.

In the world as a whole the normal effect of high tariffs is quite simple. They are like the natural impediments to transport of mountain ranges and so on; that is, they make it more difficult and more expensive to exchange the products of widely sundered regions. There is thus a continual race between improvements in the means of transport which overcome these natural impediments, and trade barriers which put others in their place. If, for example, France and England constructed a Channel Tunnel and then each stopped all additional goods passing from one country to the other by prohibitions or prohibitive tariffs, the only result of the tunnel would be to make the channel crossing more comfortable for bad sailors at the cost of the capital expended; the economic life of both countries would be substantially what it was before.

Tariffs, however, if they are reasonably stable and uniform, are at least no worse than natural obstacles. Industry and trade can be adapted to them. It is when they change unexpectedly and nobody knows what is going to happen next that they are not only injurious but destructive. They are then not like an ordinary mountain range, but a volcanic range, liable to rise and subside at any moment—across which, of course, no railway could be built. The first necessity for industry and trade organization is that they should know what conditions they have to meet. And this requires a common basis of world commercial policy. Remember that every import is somebody's export; every import shut out is an export shut in; everyone can play that game, and when a competitive policy of exclusion is started there is no natural end to it except either international agreement or a restriction of world trade to those few articles which can be neither dispensed with nor produced at home.

All that I have said so far would have been equally true last century. But the clash between frontiers and trade has become much greater in recent years because of the particular way in which modern industry is developing. More and more the great basic industries find that the most economical production is a large-scale organization. But large-scale organization needs large markets; in any but the greatest countries, like the United States of America, it is only possible if there is secure entry into much larger markets than are comprised within national frontiers. *Free* entry is not essential, but *secure* entry is. This means that if tariffs are not only high but liable to sudden increase—as tariffs now are—smaller countries are under a hopeless handicap as compared with larger ones.

This is the principal cause of the greater normal prosperity of the United States of America. America has an area there of complete and secure free trade which comprises 120 million consumers. Every manufacturer, when he is planning his organization and deciding what kind of plant to install, has the great advantage of being absolutely assured that, over this huge market no competitor will have an advantage over himself. No smaller country can give an equal advantage. It must have exports if it is to have manufacture on the largest scale, and exports may always be stopped by the action of others.

It is this economic advantage of large markets, under modern conditions, that has made the United States of America more prosperous. It supplies the motive force for the movement for a United States of Europe, and for all the efforts at Geneva of recent years to reduce and stabilize tariffs by concerted agreement.

To secure a world economic policy which gives a reasonably stable foundation for world trade is perhaps the most intricate and the most difficult task of world government. And we shall learn a great deal about the whole problem of world government if we understand how it is being attempted and why success has not yet been attained.

Let us look at this experiment; and at each point see what it teaches us about the general principles of world government. The World Economic Conference of 1927 laid it down that "tariffs while within the sovereign jurisdiction of the separate States are not of purely domestic interest." This means that a State cannot be coerced into changing its tariffs, but that it may reasonably be expected to consult with other countries whose interests are affected before taking its decision and to try to work out an agreed policy of mutual advantage.

Geneva tries to arrange this. But it does not do so by setting up some new external authority. It merely provides a mechanism through which the different countries try to agree themselves on a common policy. All the League Committees and Conferences are formed on this principle. They do not consist of international officials but of people who come from the national capitals. Officials and ministers of the Board of Trade work with similar people from other countries.

There are several advantages in this method. First no plan is started until the people best qualified to judge in London, Paris, Berlin, and so on are convinced that it is a promising one. Then the persons engaged in framing and administering commercial policy in their own capitals are brought into personal contact. They understand, as they could in no other way, just how other people are affected by what they do and how others are likely to retort if they embark on certain courses of policy. Thirdly, when a plan is arrived at, it is reached by agreement and not by external compulsion, and is therefore more likely to be acceptable and observed. And lastly the same people who have adopted it as members of an international committee or conference will carry it through in their respective countries. This means in effect that the real international organization is not a de-nationalized secretariat; it consists of the national administrations themselves linked together for an international purpose. It also means that international policy penetrates inside the life and action of the different countries as it would never do if pressed upon them by an external authority.

This is certainly the right method of international

administration. And everyone who is concerned with the problem of world government in every sphere has much to learn from it. But it has only been very partially successful. And there is just as much to learn from its failures as from its successes. Why has it been impossible to arrive at an agreed world policy about tariffs?

The first reason is that when the discussions started each country not only had its own policy, but this policy had been long put into operation; it was the basis upon which each national economic structure had been built up; it was fortified by every kind of vested interest. Any change which would injure these interests, however much it might be in the general good, was extremely difficult. If countries were starting with a clean slate to construct their commercial policy, agreement would be comparatively easy. This has never been possible. Even when everyone knows that a particular scheme started by a Government is an extremely foolish one—I could quote many instances if I were sufficiently indiscreet—you cannot change it without dismissing men from employment and wasting expensive plant. The great difficulty is that when tariffs of whatever kind have been long in operation, they have become an integral part of the national structure, and cannot be substantially changed without far-reaching consequences that few Governments are willing to face.

What general conclusion for world government are we to draw? It is this: that whenever possible world policy on a given subject needs to be formed by negotiation between the different States while national policy is still plastic—not when it has already been put into operation and it has become hard and unyielding.

The second reason for comparative failure in trying to get a world common economic policy is no less instructive. When particular interests find that they can at the general expense get a special protection for themselves if they can only persuade the Government, it becomes worth while for them to organize themselves for the purpose. This profoundly affects the whole political life of a country. Government tends to become more and more a shuttle-cock between opposing pressures. It is unable to form a deliberate policy of its own based on a general view of the national interest. After several years of trying to understand what was in the minds of the negotiators at Geneva I came to this conclusion. They were not usually thinking of a general conception of policy which they believed would be in their country's interest. They were making calculations about political pressures and reactions. What would this group of members of Parliament do if they agreed to that? If they accepted this proposal, what would be the effect on such and such trade organizations? And so on. In other words a main reason why the representatives of one country could not agree with those of others was that they were not masters in their own houses.

From this we must draw a very important general

conclusion for world government. It is this. That a strong and obstinate national representative is sometimes an obstacle to international agreements; but the worst obstacle of all is a weak representative who is afraid of his own home opinion and cannot move it however much he may be convinced himself. International organization can never be stronger than the national organizations which constitute it. Governments must govern well at home before they can govern well collectively.

The third reason why success has not been attained is that only a part of the world was negotiating at Geneva; but the problem discussed was essentially a world one. At the so-called Tariff Truce Conference, for example, it was practically only Europe that was present. But every country found it more difficult to agree not to increase its tariffs if America was not a party to the agreement.

The general conclusion to draw from this is that international government must be based on a foundation as broad as that of the activities with which it deals. And in economic and financial questions, and many others, this means that it must have a world basis.

We have seen how the clash of world trade and national frontiers involves economic loss. We have seen how necessary is a stable world commercial policy. This can only be obtained by agreement. It is an intricate and difficult task. It needs a continuous, supple, and flexible instrument of negotiation. This is best formed, as it is at Geneva, by bringing together, under a regular procedure, the representatives and officials of the different countries in direct, frequent, and intimate contact. But it cannot be successful unless, as has not hitherto been the case, national policy is reasonably adjustable, national Governments are masters in their own home, and not the slaves of organized pressure, and unless all the countries principally concerned are participants. The opportunity for restarting on better lines may soon occur again—and must do so unless the world decides to relinquish the enormous advantages of a prosperous world trade. The reward of success is not only greater prosperity, but the removal of the greatest of all dangers to the peace of the world.

Mankind is continuously engaged in a struggle to earn the necessities of life, and to add luxuries to these necessities. The forces generated by this struggle are the strongest in the world. If the clash and conflict with national frontiers continually increase; if the great tides of the world's economic life are more and more deflected from their natural course; if each country acts without consultation with others or consideration of their interests, without any concerted basis of policy or agreed principles—the end is sooner or later inevitable.

This does not mean either that complete freedom of trade is essential or that countries must relinquish their sovereignties. But it does mean that we must establish some form of world government which secures a sufficient basis of agreement to prevent perpetual dislocation and perpetual friction.

3. NATIONAL SOVEREIGNTY AND WORLD PEACE

I HAVE discussed how industry and trade now look to world markets; and how they are brought into conflict with national laws and national frontiers. This clash between world trade and national frontiers always causes loss, confusion, and friction. Wherever, indeed, any of man's activities have thus acquired a world range, and at the same time are governed by conflicting national regulations, loss and friction of this kind are inevitable. And so many activities are now of this character that the question is naturally asked whether we must not abolish national sovereignty and substitute a supreme world authority if we are to preserve good international relations and peace. Mr. H. G. Wells, for example, urges that national sovereignty must go. This is the question I now propose to discuss.

We must first try to make a picture to ourselves of the main framework of government in the world. Let me suggest an image. You know the ingenious toy called a Chinese box. You have a small square box enclosed in a larger one; this second box is inside one still larger and so on. So that you may have perhaps a dozen boxes, one inside the other, one big box enclosing the whole, while each of the twelve boxes can be taken out and used separately. Now in the nature of the case government must be rather like that. There are local affairs, and national affairs, and world affairs. Each requires an appropriate organ of government; and it must be possible, in each case, to act separately for certain purposes. But at the same time the separate action must, at the appropriate stage, fit in with that of the wider and superior authority. Thus we have Parish Councils and County Councils; and then the national organ: the Parliament and Cabinet. Finally, we have the beginning of world government in the League of Nations, wider than any national government in the geographical area of its authority, but restricted in its range of subjects and its actual power.

Now in this expanding series of public authorities one is of altogether outstanding importance. It is the National Government. In this country, this consists of Parliament, which comprises the King, his ministers, the House of Lords, and the House of Commons. Parliament in this wide sense is supreme in the country. It determines the scope of authority within which every lesser authority works, and it makes the laws under which we all conduct our business. No other authority is in this sense supreme. In some countries, however, such as the United States of America and Switzerland, there is a Federal system of government under which separate States or Cantons are similarly supreme within limits determined not by the Federal Parliament but by a written constitution. And in a few, but very few, cases, the supremacy of the national authority is subject to an overriding world authority. Under the Covenant of the League of Nations, for example, an individual country no longer has the right to resort to War without notice, or to enforce a claim unanimously rejected by the States who constitute the Council of the League.

With few exceptions, however, the national authority can legally do anything it likes. It can prescribe what subordinate authorities are to do. It is rarely, except with its own consent, under an obligation to do what any wider authority may desire. It has in its hands the material power to maintain and enforce the rights; a police to enforce its laws and regulations at home; and an armed force to resist aggression or compulsion from abroad. This, shortly, is what we mean by national sovereignties. They are under present conditions the real units of government in the world.

In practice, of course, the theoretically almost unlimited supreme power of national sovereignties is restricted in several ways. Within each country, public opinion, based on deeply rooted traditions, sets limits to what the national Governments can do and indeed in most cases the public forms and changes that Government by election.

Externally, treaties, customs, understandings, and rules of behaviour, termed "International Law," set limits upon the action of an individual country. And protests from other Governments, enforced in the last resort by the threat or use of military action, normally secure the observance of these limits. It remains true, however, that in the expanding series of the instruments of Governments, the national Government is still by far the most important and the most powerful. This is due to the fact that Nations, in addition to being legally sovereign, enjoy and employ two rights of special importance, that of raising national armies and that of enforcing national commercial policies, chiefly in the form of tariffs; and that national Governments are based upon a stronger force of public opinion than any others. Let us consider first this last point.

We have spoken of an expanding series of governing authorities. We must remember that these have their counterpart in an expanding series of individual loyalties. A man lives in a particular village or town or borough, which in turn is in a particular county; he is next a citizen of a particular country; and lastly, he is a citizen of the world. To all these he owes and gives loyalties of varying intensities. He has in addition, of course, a whole series of further loyalties which are not related directly to organs of public government. He is a member of a family, of a school, a business, a religion, and perhaps a dozen or more associations which represent his personal tastes and interests. These different loyalties are not in their nature inconsistent or in conflict. On the contrary, each of them may strengthen the others. A man is not a worse, but a better, citizen

because he is devoted to his family; he is likely to
serve his country better, and not worse, because he
gives public service to his town council. In just the
same way he may be a good citizen of the world
without ceasing to be a good patriot.

But it is also clear that each of these loyalties
may be in conflict with the others if it is excessive,
disproportionate, or unreasonable. A devoted citizen
of Liverpool, for example, would be a bad citizen
of his country if he insisted that the Liverpool City
Council should never employ men from other parts
of England.

The problem of government is to make each
part of the expanding series of public authorities
correspond with the character of the activities it
has to regulate. The psychological problem of the
individual citizen is to adjust each of his loyalties
so that they do not injure the others. Now, if we take
only those loyalties which relate to government,
it will be clear that national government has the
greatest advantage.

Most men think of themselves more as Englishmen
than as citizens of London, Birmingham, or Manchester.

This was not always so. In about the fourteenth
century, for example, men's most passionate loyalties
were both wider and narrower than the nation.
They thought of themselves as members of the
Catholic Church on the one hand or devoted to
a particular city or territorial chief on the other.

Public authority corresponded with these loyalties. The Catholic Church was more powerful than national sovereigns. The Duke of Burgundy enjoyed more power and could call more upon loyalty than a weak national King. Men thought of themselves as Catholics or Burgundians more than as Frenchmen. The extreme intensities of national feelings and the extreme development of the power of the national sovereignties are indeed much more recent than this. The last century, even the last half century, since the rise of Prussia, has witnessed a great increase in both. And, of course, all national and nationalistic feeling has recently been inflamed by four years of war in which every belligerent country naturally did what it could to intensify these feelings in order to maintain the will to fight.

We have, then, in the intensity of national feeling, and in the character of national government, something that is excessive and abnormal by the standard of the past. What is much more important, it is inconvenient by the test of what the present activities of the world require. What is now happening on a wider scale is well illustrated by what happened in the reform of London Government by the creation of the London County Council. London grew up out of separate boroughs or small towns which gradually ran into each other. For a long time after London had become a single unit as far as the life and work of its inhabitants were concerned, it was governed by many separate authorities whose action came into conflict with each other. When people live in Streatham, work in the City, have their friends in Hampstead, or Battersea, or Ealing, and go for their amusements to Westminster or Holborn, it becomes excessively inconvenient if the different borough authorities control not only local but common services as well. The trams, and roads, and drainage system, and schools of a single great community cannot be properly run under little local authorities.

This is now what is happening in a wider sphere as a larger and larger proportion of man's activities take a world range, while Government remains predominantly national. Confusion, loss—and above all increasing friction—are bound to result. And the friction is much more dangerous because each of these national Governments has armed forces under its orders. If Balham quarrelled with Brixton last century, nobody expected that either would try to win its case by ordering the local police to fight. But if Germany quarrels with France, this danger is at once imminent.

Must we then abolish national sovereignty if we are to preserve peace? Must we aim at the immediate establishment of a supreme super-State, or at least at a World Federation, under which National Governments will be reduced to the status of County Councils—or, at least, of the separate States in such a country as the U.S.A.

Ultimately I believe a World Federation must

come, as the life of the world becomes essentially international and as more and more of our activities take a world range. This does not, of course, mean that even then there will not be National Governments or that we shall cease to think of ourselves as Frenchmen and Englishmen. But it does mean that National Governments would only be supreme within defined limits of action; in others the World Federal Government would be sovereign. And it also means, if it is to be securely established, that men of different countries must think of themselves primarily as citizens of the world rather than as Englishmen or Frenchmen, just as a man living in London now thinks of himself more as an Englishman than as a Londoner. Now it is going to be a long time before we think of ourselves as citizens of the world first and citizens of England second. This second condition, therefore, shows how difficult it would be to make *such* a change of government—and how long it will take.

If world peace is going to be always in danger until we have established a World Federation, supreme over National Governments, then we must all, I fear, expect to live in this danger for the greater part of our lives. Whatever be the final goal, cannot we establish a sure basis of peace with a less drastic reform?

I believe we can. A form of world government much more restricted in extent and much more modest in nature would, I think, relieve us from both the loss and the danger involved in independent national sovereignty.

First as to extent—that is, the range of act.vities affected. It is only in two spheres that conflicting national action involves serious loss or real danger: economic and financial policy on the one hand and foreign policy, with the military preparations that are a counterpart of it, on the other.

We can, indeed, make the limits even narrower. Within economics and finance the real danger comes from competitive and conflicting commercial policies. It is not the right to tax, or to adopt differing systems for the management of industry, that causes danger. It is the right to erect tariffs. In the other sphere, foreign policy is now to a large extent formed by negotiation through a world organ of government; we need only to develop this; the real danger is the right to raise, without limit, national armed forces which are a threat to other countries.

The extension to other spheres of world government might be convenient; it might or might not be desirable. Uniformity in divorce laws, or systems of taxation; or regulations governing foreign travel or residence might be an advantage. But in these matters absence of uniformity does not threaten peace.

It is two attributes of national sovereignty, and two only, that cause a danger of war; the right to erect tariffs, without regard to the economic loss they inflict on others, and the right to raise armies without regard to the danger they involve for others.

We can therefore concentrate our attention on tariffs and armaments. And even here we need not contemplate anything so drastic as the abolition either of tariffs or armaments; or the substitution of an external world authority to settle what these shall be. It will be enough if national governments will, in both cases, voluntarily restrict the exercise of their independent right of action by durable agreements.

We can, for example, imagine a Tariff convention under which all countries would agree that for a specified and substantial period they will limit their duties on the various categories of goods to defined amounts; that they will not increase them without notice and consultation; and that they will gradually, and equally, proceed with a co-ordinated policy, designed to reduce the impediments to world trade.

Such a convention, based upon a voluntary agreement and leaving freedom of action within the limits thus voluntarily accepted, would not involve an abolition of national sovereignties nor rouse in opposition the feelings which support national sovereignties. At the same time it would greatly reduce the economic loss caused by tariffs as they now are and almost entirely get rid of the friction and danger by which they are now attended.

So too as regards armaments. If the different

countries would agree upon a convention which would restore national armaments and military forces to a level at which they no longer cause apprehension, and make it certain that they would not be increased again above that level, we should similarly, without abolition of national sovereignty, have escaped the greater part of the economic loss and nearly all the dangers now involved in competitive armaments.

If only these two rights of sovereignties—the right to erect frontiers and the right to raise armies—could be thus restricted by agreement, we need ask no more concessions from the nationalist to assure peace for long to come. Indeed, national sentiment and patriotism, national or local desires for self-determination, could in many respects find a freer—because it will be an innocuous—expression. In general internal social and economic policy, in the development of national or local culture, in education and indeed in every other sphere of man's activities and interests, government could adapt itself to whatever the public wished. It is not an aid to really national development, but the worst of all handicaps to it, that the overhanging fear of war compels a form of national government which aims at making the whole country unite, whenever called upon, to act as a unit against other countries.

The policy I have advocated may seem to some utopian; to others too timorous. I believe it is a practicable course between an unlicensed and unregulated nationalism which must lead to war and a premature attempt at the suppression of national sovereignty which must lead to failure. Whatever be the ultimate ideal, I believe now, not in abolishing national frontiers, but in taking the poison from them by voluntary agreements as to tariff policy; I believe now, not in trying to abolish national armies, but in limiting them by progressive conventions.

And at each step, by a procedure which I have already set out when I was describing the economic work of the League, I believe that we should work out the agreements through committees or conferences of national representatives. By this method we can go just as far as the state of public opinion in each country allows us without the certain result of a destructive reaction. In other words, I think we should now aim not at destroying but at diluting nationalism; not at abolishing national sovereignty but at restricting its exercise by successive voluntary agreements; not at creating some new external organ of world government, but (as the League does) at helping the nations of the world to govern themselves by agreement and by convention.

World government in a fuller sense may come, must come, ultimately: but it will be the better— and the safer—if it is built up gradually, in this way, each stage being consolidated, tested, and fortified in practice before the next is attempted.

4. WORLD GOVERNMENT

WE have seen how world government has become necessary because the range of many of men's activities has become world-wide and we have had illustrations showing how this world government is being built up. What is being done is not to try to create some new external authority, but to link together the national governments of the world so that for certain purposes they can act as a single world government. This is the fundamental principle of the League of Nations, of which the governing authorities, the Assembly and the Council, consist of the national representatives of the governments of the different Member States. When the League is dealing with political questions, the Foreign Ministers of the national governments constitute the Council; when a League Conference conducts economic or financial negotiations, it is composed of representatives of the different Boards of Trade or Treasuries.

Any other way of trying to make a world government would, under present circumstances, be both impracticable and useless. We could not, if we wished, set up some new external world authority with power to override national governments, and if we could set it up it would certainly break down. National governments would never agree to such a new authority being set over themselves and the peoples of nearly every country would support them in resisting such a proposal. And even if by a miracle they were got to agree, it is certain that when this new authority tried to act it would find itself impotent.

Suppose, for example, that a new world authority were set up, composed of some of the best and wisest people in the world, but without governmental position in their own countries; let us imagine that this authority decided that world tariffs ought to be reduced by 10 per cent, or that no increase should be made for a year, how could it secure that practical effect was given to this decision? Each national government can enact a new tariff through its own parliament, can apply it through its customs officials, can enforce it through its police and, in the last resort, has its army to prevent any external interference. It is essential, therefore, that the organs of a world government, such as the Assembly and Council of the League, should consist of people who represent national governments, who can within the limits of a more or less elastic delegated authority negotiate with other countries and, when they agree, can secure that their national governments act in accordance with their agreements.

It is very important to realize this. Many progressive people, impatient with the slow progress of existing governments, have advocated that the Assembly of the League of Nations should, as they say, represent the peoples and not the governments of the world. If they got their way, and if the Assembly were in fact composed each year of people not representing, but more progressive than, the national governments, what would be the result? We should get resolutions that internationalists might think very much better than the resolutions we are now getting, but they would be subject to the fatal defect that they would begin and end as resolutions. They would not compel action.

We have to face the plain fact that if we want a particular kind of policy pursued, we must in our own countries elect the kind of government which will support it. After all, so far as the nations of the world have free and democratic constitutions, the Assembly of the League, by being composed of representatives of national governments, is automatically representative of the peoples of the world. It is representative through the regular constitutional and effective process of taking people who have been elected in their own countries. It is useless to attempt to short-circuit this normal and proper process.

You may say, however, "If all the League does is to secure that national governments consult together while leaving each of them with its full and independent sovereign power as before, what has it done? Governments have always consulted together, either by conferences or diplomatic communications, on matters which were of common concern. What, then, is the meaning of saying that the League represents the beginning of a real world government?" Let me, in reply, sum up the differences between the League method and the old method of diplomatic communications and special conferences.

In the first place, under the League system, governments now meet at regular periods and under a regular procedure. This regularity of meeting links the governments as no series of improvised conferences would ever do.

In the second place, this frequent personal contact of the representative ministers of the different countries builds up a basis of mutual personal understanding and often personal friendship, which adds greatly to the foundations upon which common action must be built. No communication in writing or through ambassadors or any occasional conference would ever have the same effect.

In the third place, the permanent machinery of the League, in existence before the ministers meet and remaining when they have parted, secures that the work is prepared on an international basis and that the decisions when taken are executed.

Fourthly, the same principle of regular personal contact is applied not only to the meetings of foreign ministers on the Council or in the Assembly, it is applied also to a whole network of specialized committees extending over every sphere of economic or financial or social and other questions in which co-ordinated action between different countries is necessary. Each set of problems is represented by a regular meeting of people who are in the best position to influence the action in these countries.

Lastly, and most important of all, when Foreign Ministers meet regularly in the Council of the League, they become more than national ministers advocating national policies. They have a second capacity. The Council becomes more than a committee of negotiators. It acquires a personality and traditions of its own. Its policy is built out of national policies but it becomes more than the mere sum of these policies or a compromise between them. A new element, constituted of the international aspect of each member thus sitting in a dual capacity, is added. At the same time, the clash between world government and national government is avoided. If the French, British, and German Ministers assent as Members of the Council to policy which requires action by each of their Governments, they carry out this action as members of those Governments. They, and their Governments, and their countries behind them, become part of the living tissue of a world organism.

This, then, is the real machinery of the world government as it exists at present. It consists essentially of using the national governments and the national administrations and so linking them together that they can act for a common purpose.

It has also one other effect. Several thousands of people, each of them a person of influence in one capacity or another in his own country, are each year brought together in direct contact. They learn each other's point of view; they take back to their own country a world point of view. Under this system, therefore, not only does the power and experience of the administrative machine of each national country help to give effect to the policy of world government, but the thought and action of each national country are also permeated with a world point of view.

In this way world government is being built up and must be built up. It is of the essence of it that the national governments are units of world government. Each stone in the world structure is a national stone.

If, then, national governments are the units of world government, we must enquire what these national units are, how many there are, what are their differences, what are their special characteristics, and what are the difficulties in the task of constructing from them a world government.

These questions are not easy to answer. It is not easy to say even how many national governments we must regard as units of world government. There are hundreds of countries or political units of one kind and another in the world with separate governments. In the British Empire alone, for example (apart from India and the British Dominions, to which I will refer in a moment), there are perhaps fifty or so colonies, each with its own government, with different degrees of local representation and different relations to the central British Government. All these, however, we can for our present purpose set aside. We need not take them as primary units in the world government, since for the purpose of world government we can look to the British Government as representing them; they are not sovereign and independent.

Let us now turn to India. Here is another problem. India consists of two parts—British India and the Indian States. The Indian States are ruled by some hundred of native princes and rulers of differing power and authority, who are formally not subject to the British Government, but allies of H.M. the King. Here again, however, for the practical purpose of world government, it is possible to secure that India as a whole is regarded as a single unit.

Consider now the British Dominions. Here we have the opposite difficulty. They are not formally and legally separate sovereign states in the same full sense as, say, France and Germany are. They all owe allegiance to the same king, but whereas the sovereignty of the Indian princes is more formal than real, that of the British Dominions is more real than formal; they determine their own policy. They must therefore be regarded, as they are in the League constitution, as separate units in world government.

There is another class of difficulty. There are quite a number of little constitutional accidents or anomalies in the world—little communities with a population and a power no greater than those comprised in the area of many municipal authorities, who are yet formally and legally independent. There is the little State of Liechtenstein and the little Republic of Andorra in the Pyrenees on the borders of France and Spain. There is the little Principality of Monaco, which for most international purposes does not need to be separately represented from France. These again we need not consider as separate units in our world structure. Those who framed the League of Nations had to face this problem. They took a practical criterion of eligibility to membership of the League; they rejected small sovereign States like Andorra while admitting to separate membership self-governing dominions under a single sovereign like Australia and Canada. There are between sixty and seventy states in the world which would be eligible for membership of the League in this way. These include the U.S.A., the U.S.S.R., Turkey, which are not members of the League, some countries in South America which alternate between membership and resignation, and a few other countries.

To establish the units of world government is, however, only the first step. It is obviously extremely difficult to weld into a single instrument of government national governments which vary so widely in size, in their constitutional forms and traditions, and represent peoples of such differing culture and civilization as do the sixty to seventy eligible for League membership.

Let us look at some of these differences and of the special problems they create when we are trying to build a world government.

Take size to start with. You have a country as big as China with four hundred millions, one-fifth of the whole world's population, and then you have Switzerland with 3 to 4 millions only, and other States smaller still. Consider the enormous differences of civilization, of culture, of religion, and traditional outlook and policy. You have on the one hand the immemorial civilization of the East, and on the other the miraculously rapid occidental civilization of the United States.

Then again, even in countries of similar culture, there is the greatest possible difference in the basis of national authority. There is the free elective Republic of France next door to the Dictatorship of Italy. There is again every kind of variation in the degree of authority with which representatives of a given State can negotiate. This is often the cause of great misunderstanding and confusion. When, for example, France and Great Britain signed the Treaty of Versailles, everybody assumed—and the assumption was justified—that the national parliaments would at once ratify. It came as a surprise to many when the American signature was not similarly endorsed. This surprise, even accompanied by indignation, was largely due to the fact that most of us who live under other forms of constitution do not understand how essentially different is a federal written constitution like that of the United States. We forget that the United States were formed into a single entity on the basis of a written constitution, whose primary object was to maintain for ever the independent rights of the constituent States. The whole American Constitution from beginning to end is founded upon the principle of a careful safe-guarding of each section of the country and of its government machine from encroachment by the others. The States are safeguarded against the overriding authority of the Federal Government; the two Houses of Congress are safeguarded against any overriding authority of the President and his ministers. The Senate expects to be much more than a ratifying and approving body; it expects in negotiations of foreign policy to be an active parti-cipant. This is why we hear so much of Senator Borah, who is not a minister but Chairman of the Senate's Foreign Affairs Committee. In constrast with this, most European constitutions have grown up under the ever-present necessity of so organizing the country that it could negotiate and deal with foreign countries.

Let us take yet another difference. Governments differ enormously in the extent to which they can in fact govern and control the people within their nominal sovereign jurisdiction. This is one of the great underlying difficulties in the Far Eastern situation at this moment. China is the greatest country in the world, but the Chinese Government is one of the weakest. Sometimes again there is an internal division in the authority of a national government which is very difficult for other countries to appreciate and may at any moment have most important consequences. The Far Eastern situation again illustrates this particular difficulty. No one will understand that position if he does not bear in mind that the heads of the fighting services in Japan are not responsible, as they are in most countries with an electoral system, to the Prime Minister and the civil government; they have a direct and separate responsibility to the Emperor and, as we have seen, they can sometimes take direct initiative of the first importance without the control of the civil government.

It can be readily understood how difficult it is to build up a structure of world government out of constituent elements so different as these. It is rather like having to build, let us say, a House of Parliament out of all the chance materials of a builder's yard, which included the material for every kind of building, from a cathedral to a cottage.

We shall never understand what is the real task of making a world government unless we always have in our minds a vivid picture of the immense variety of national governments in the world and of the countries and peoples and civilizations for whose destinies they are responsible.

5. REFEREE OR SUPERSTATE?

How can World Government be made fit for its task?

We have seen how a new world government is being built up. It is not a new external government, a new superstate. It is composed of the national governments; and its councils, conferences, and committees consist of national representatives and national experts. This government has its headquarters at Geneva, where it uses the mechanism of a permanent secretariat. I want now to discuss how this new world government can be developed and improved.

The first necessity is that for questions that are really world questions in the fullest sense, this new world government must be equally world-wide in its composition and authority. Several great countries, in particular the United States of America and Russia, are of course not members of the League of Nations. For many questions, however, this defect is easily overcome. When the League is dealing with disarmament, for example, America and Russia both become full members of the Disarmament Conference. In most of the Committees of the League, which deal with economic, financial, and social questions, again, there are American members on the appropriate committees. It would, however, greatly facilitate the work on these subjects if these arrangements were regularized, and if, at least for this purpose, America and Russia were, so to speak, regular members of the League, paying definite contribution and regarding themselves as present on just the same terms as other nationalities. This they could do without accepting the political engagements of the League, which constitute the real difficulty in their ratifying the Covenant.

Even then, however, there would remain the great political problem of maintaining the peace of the world—the first duty of the League and the first necessary condition and basis of all world government. It is more and more evident that wars originate in world causes; that when they break out anywhere, they tend to spread everywhere; that their consequences are world-wide; and lastly, and most important of all, that it is only by a collective world influence that the serious danger arising from a quarrel between two great countries can be averted. The crisis in the Far East is an illustration of this. Even the collective influence of the whole world is barely sufficient to deal with that crisis. If the world is divided, or if it has no methods by which it can effectively co-operate, failure must be expected. And this is true of all the greatest dangers of the future that are to be anticipated.

It is vital, therefore, that the great countries which are not now members of the League should be a real part of world government and of the world peace machinery.

This does not, however, necessarily mean that peace cannot be assured unless America and Russia join the League of Nations. Both these great countries have signed the Pact of Paris (commonly known as the Kellogg Pact), together with other countries like our own, which are members of the League of Nations. This Kellogg Pact is not an alternative or a rival to the League; it supplements it. Its great defect, if it stands by itself, is that it has no machinery through which to assure effect for its principles, and, in particular, for its main principle that all countries stand together in renouncing war as an instrument of national policy. If America is determined to make this Kellogg Pact a reality; is prepared to consult and co-operate with other countries who have signed the Pact when any difficulty arises; and is ready to do so in a way which does not impair the working of the League machinery for its own members but supplements it, the problem might be solved. The Kellogg Pact and the Covenant, linked together; the one reinforcing the other; the first bringing its wider range of membership and the second making available its permanent machinery, might become in effect a single instrument for the purpose of securing a peaceful settlement of disputes and averting war.

If this were done, I believe that the present still imperfect world government at Geneva could be made in the fullest sense a world authority for questions that need such an authority for their settlement.

If, however, the League is not big enough in its membership for some questions, it is too big and too cumbrous for others. In its present form it is an incomplete world authority. But a great many of the actual problems of the day, while international, are essentially localized. It is a very cumbrous thing to bring in nearly every country in the world when you are dealing with questions that only affect a few countries. Some questions are European only; others affect a particular region, perhaps the Danubian provinces; in other cases the Far East or South America may be directly concerned. It is, I think, essential that· for regional questions of this kind the world authority should develop a regional machinery. In fact, it is beginning to do so.

When, for example, the League dealt with the reconstruction of Hungary, it recognized that certain countries had a specially strong interest not shared equally by the rest of the world. It formed, therefore, a special Standing Committee consisting of Hungary herself, Great Britain, France, Italy, and, among Hungary's neighbours, Czechoslovakia, Roumania, and Jugoslavia. This Committee remained in existence during all the years the reconstruction work was in progress, and thus became for a substantial period an addition to the constitution of the League. The same procedure was adopted in the case of the reconstruction of Austria and the settlement of refugees in Bulgaria.

A more important instance of the same principle is the establishment of the European Commission, under the late Monsieur Briand's initiative, for attempting to promote greater economic and political unity in Europe. The danger, however, in the case of so large a group within the League as one which covers the whole of Europe (particularly while the greatest of the non-European countries is not a member of the League), is that it tends to overbalance the League as a whole. For it is, of course, of the most vital importance that a world authority should, as a world authority, be supreme over any smaller group within it. However localized a question is, and however convenient it may be that it should for the most part be dealt with by groups of countries and not by them all; it always necessarily touches world interests at one point or another. The League has therefore very wisely adopted the principle that every local or regional group within it should receive its mandate of authority from the League as a whole and should periodically report to the full League authorities, the Council and the Assembly. The world authority thus has a watching brief, and is enabled to intervene if local settlements are contemplated at the expense of countries who are not parties to them.

The most important thing of all, however, in order that world government may be made a reality, is that the different governments of the world and their peoples behind them should in every possible respect *make* it a reality by using it and conducting their negotiations through it.

You often hear it said that discussions at Geneva are unreal, and that if you want business the governments must deal with each other through the old political channels. The fact is that the discussions are just as real as the national governments make them, and the usefulness of any decision arrived at at Geneva depends upon the extent to which those decisions embody the result of the real negotiations between the countries concerned. If, as sometimes happens, the principal Powers send their representatives to Geneva to discuss a current problem and then leave them with few instructions (and sometimes inadequate information) while they negotiate with each other through other channels, the result must of course be that what happens at Geneva is unreal and without value. That, however, is the fault not of Geneva but of the Great Powers.

In the second place, it is very important that the different countries should actually build up their policy in each sphere of international action through the machinery of the League. If each country works out its policy at home to the last detail and then throws it at the heads of the others at Geneva, anything like a satisfactory world policy will be almost impossible. That is what America and Great Britain did with their plans for the Naval Conference of 1927; and that is largely why that Conference failed. Differing national policies need to be brought into contact with each other while they are still to a large extent plastic.

So far it will be seen that the kind of world government which I have been describing is essentially *international* government, not *superstate* government: that is, the nations frame their policy by voluntary agreement; they do not have decisions imposed upon them. Let me discuss this difference.

International government is based upon agreement at every stage between the different countries. No country under such a system relinquishes any part of its independent sovereignty. It merely, by a voluntary act, restricts the exercise of its sovereignty in a given sphere and perhaps for a given time. World government only begins to acquire something of the character of a superstate just to the extent to which (in place of voluntary agreement at every stage) a particular country or minority can be overridden by some kind of majority vote. The League almost without exception is based on the first principle. It requires unanimity for nearly all its decisions. This need to secure unanimity is obviously a very important limiting factor. But on the whole those who have watched the system working have probably been surprised that it is not more of a decisive impediment to progress than it has been. The feeling that a result must be reached; the collective power of a considerable majority, when it exists, to *persuade* the minority is in fact very great; and when agreement can be reached in this way the results are more securely established than if they had been obtained by an overriding of a minority by a majority.

There are two cases, however, in which the League does just begin to partake of the character of a superstate, though only within very modest limits. In the first place, every country which has ratified the Covenant has definitely agreed for ever not to make war to enforce a claim which has been unanimously rejected as unjust by all the countries on the Council of the League, except the countries involved in the dispute. This is an instance in which the League has legal authority without having to secure complete unanimity. In the second place, for the smooth working of the League machinery it has been necessary to give power to a majority to decide on questions of procedure, e.g. whether a particular committee should be appointed and so on. These are, it will be seen, very modest and elementary extensions of the normal principle that unanimity is necessary for decision and that therefore the League is in its essence international and not super-national.

While I think that this international principle, based upon unanimity, is the right foundation of world government, I also think that very gradually there must be some development in the direction of limited super-government. In other words, I think that, as the real activities of the world become more and more international, there should, in time, be some way of securing majority decisions. We must recognize, however, that this at once raises very great difficulties.

The first is that of voting power. This difficulty arises from the enormous difference between the size and importance of the different countries which, as we saw in our last talk, are units of world government. If there is to be a majority voting power, there must be some form of franchise. For the purpose of deciding procedure, this is unimportant. It does not matter that, for such a purpose, a country of the size of Switzerland should have the same vote as France. Nor does this difficulty arise in the other case I have mentioned, viz. the right of the Council as a whole to impose its will upon the two disputants in a particular quarrel; for there it is not really a majority vote, but a unanimous vote with the exception of the two interested countries. But directly the world authority should desire to decide questions of policy affecting the action or interests of the different sovereign governments, this question of voting power becomes of fundamental importance. Unless it can be solved, no progress can be made in that direction.

At this point I must remark that there is often great confusion in the use of the phrase at Geneva "All States are equal." If this means that a small State has the same right to justice as a large State, it is obviously sound. It is in fact one of the great merits of the League that it sets out to secure a settlement on the merits of any dispute between two countries, even the largest and the smallest, without allowing the weaker to be overborne in negotiations, as in the past, by greater strength.

If, however, we mean, by the equality of all States, that each State should have an equal voice in determining upon world policy, the principle would be obvious nonsense. It would involve a direct penalty to the citizens of every great country in proportion to its size. France, for example, has a population about six times as great as that of Belgium, and, being of a similar civilization, has a correspondingly greater importance as a unit in the world. If, therefore, France and Belgium were each to have an equal vote in determining policy that affects the interests and actions of each of them, this would mean in effect that the average Belgian was exercising six times as great a power as the average Frenchman. This would obviously be unjust. The difficulty cannot, however, be solved merely on a population basis. It would be quite as absurd to give, let us say, China ten times as many votes in determining world policy as France as it would be to give Belgium an equal vote with France.

Somehow or other this problem of franchise will have to be solved if world government ever needs to assume something of the character of super-government for certain classes of questions.

I believe myself that the solution will ultimately be on the lines of a classification of countries under

certain great categories, based upon actual importance in world policy and actual range of world
interests. This in turn would depend partly upon
population, partly upon wealth and strength, partly
upon range of national activities. The difficulty of
classification would of course be great. But I do not
believe it would be ultimately insuperable. You have
the beginnings of such a classification in the distinction between the Great Powers, who are permanent members of the Council of the League of
Nations, and other countries who are not. A further
intermediate class is developing of countries like
Poland and Spain, which are beginning to be
recognized as eligible for re-election after their
normal term of office on the Council; that is to say,
a new class of what are popularly called "semi-
permanent" members of the League is being created.
I believe that ultimately, if the world does move
towards limited super-government, the problem of
franchise will be solved along these lines. That,
however, is to look far ahead into the future.

For the present, world government is, and will
remain for practically all purposes, international
government based upon agreement and requiring
unanimous votes for its decisions. It is this government which we must devote our efforts to strengthen-
ing in the near future.

6. THE RIDDLE OF THE FUTURE

I WANT to attempt to look into the future and see how world government would be working if it developed as I should like to see it develop during, let us say, the next twenty-five years. I say twenty-five years because that is near enough, I hope, for most of you to compare the fact with the prophesy—and at the same time, it is long enough, I fear, to make it impossible for you to call me to account for my mistakes.

But before attempting to see what world government will be like, if we assume that it will develop as it should, I must emphasize that this is of course a doubtful assumption. The world may fail for long to come to secure the kind of government it needs. Nationalism may oppose too strong a resistance. We may have for a long period a constantly increasing clash between national frontiers and world trade. We may have many years of confusion, friction, and unnecessary loss. We may fail to avoid the shattering disaster of another great war. Or even if that is avoided, we may live under a perpetual sword of Damocles; we may fail to obtain the basis of confidence and security upon which alone the activities of the world can find their natural and normal development.

The forces that make on the one hand for world government, in which national governments shall take their proper place, and on the other hand for the continuance of competing nationalisms without the restraint of any wider authority, are not unequal. The balance, indeed, is so even that all of us have the greatest possible inducement to throw our weight upon the right side. The future of the world and of every country in it depends upon whether the balance finally turns in one direction or the other.

But let me for the moment assume the best and look into the future on that assumption. How will world government then be working in a quarter of a century's time?

Let us imagine first the mere mechanism of national co-operation. Let us picture, for example, a meeting of the Council of the League of Nations at Geneva on some afternoon in spring of the year 1957, convened to deal with some problem of outstanding interest and importance. I see, sitting round the table, the future Sir John Simon, and other future ministers of Europe. They will have come, as at present, from their respective capitals. But they will not have come as they would have done a century ago in coaches taking weeks or months, nor as they do now in a train taking a day or days. They will have flown from their capitals between breakfast and lunch.

Even so, however, the means of transport will make it difficult for the future Mr. Stimson to come himself three thousand miles, or the future President

Chang Kai Shek to come six thousand miles from China. But by that time wireless telephony will be extended and improved and we shall have television as well. I imagine, therefore, that the seat of the table reserved for the American or the Chinese representative may be occupied by a canvas screen on which the figures of the future Mr. Stimson and the future Chang Kai Shek will be shown as they are in their respective offices on the other side of the world, living and life-size. Meantime, each of them in his own distant office will have a similar picture before his face of the Council and all the living and speaking figures of those who compose it at Geneva. Thus a Council meeting will take place; a debate will proceed with the same quick rejoinder and retort that is possible when all are physically present, even though a quarter or a half of the members are in another hemisphere. The British representative at Geneva will see before him the expression on the face of the American representative in Washington caused by his own remarks a second or two earlier. The American representative in Washington in turn will not only hear but see those with whom he is debating at Geneva.

Meantime, behind the ministers sitting round the table there will be, as at present, their official advisers. Among them those who advise the distant members will have a special rôle to play. They will, in the intervals between the meetings and the speeches, be talking directly to their chiefs at home.

Wireless telephony will perhaps have become as much a part of the ordinary mechanism of discussion between distant countries as ordinary telephoning is now in London, and will no longer be an expensive luxury or a method of communication reserved for rare and desperate emergencies.

Already we see it is developing at an extraordinary pace. A substantial part, for example, of the discussions about the Far Eastern crisis have taken the form of direct personal conversations between our own ministers and ministers at Washington, and so on. But in twenty-five years we may assume that this will have gone immensely further. Conceivably also we shall then have learnt to improve selection between wave-lengths to such an extent that we shall be able to have our individual wave-lengths as we now have our individual telephone numbers, and we may perhaps be then carrying our little wireless receiving set in our waistcoat pocket as we now carry a watch.

The political authority of Geneva and the Judicial Tribunal at The Hague will between them make the law of the world and apply it. For we must never forget that the world is always changing, and that we need not only to decide what are existing legal rights, but to change them when world development requires.

So much for the mechanism of world government. Let us now consider the kind of questions it will have to deal with.

If for twenty-five years we have successfully
avoided a great war and have been making progress in eliminating the causes of war, the whole
character of future international discussion will be
different. During the last thirteen years everything
has been dominated by the embittered national
feeling inflamed by the late war and everything has
turned upon a number of embittered disputes resulting from the Treaty settlement. Perhaps many of
us have come to regard such disputes about Danzig
or the Polish Corridor, or the frontier between
Roumania and Czechoslovakia, or the connection
between Austria and Germany, as the normal sub-
stance of the life of the world. Happily, it is not
that.

If we can only progress as we should in the next
twenty-five years, all these special disputes will have
disappeared into past history, and many of the
embittered feelings that they have both expressed
and caused will have disappeared with them.
National rivalries and ambitions will still remain.
but they will be more and more like the rivalries
and ambitions between two countries or two states
in a single country. They will be of the nature of
healthy competition rather than dangerous friction.

After a long period of peace and successful working of the peace system, each government and the
public of the world will feel confident in the maintenance of peace, will take it for granted that if any
single country should threaten war the rest of the

world will unite against it. With this confidence one country after another will feel that this is the main factor in its own national security. More and more it will feel able to reduce its armed forces to the character of police forces to maintain national order. As each country gives effect to this conclusion, others will in turn feel more confident and be encouraged to proceed along the same path. We shall then have a reversal of the process which brought us the last disaster and still threatens another. We shall have a friendly competition in disarmament instead of an embittered competition in arming.

With confidence so assured, the first condition for economic development finding its fullest world range will be established. The savings of one part of the world will flow quickly, easily, cheaply, and above all regularly, in fructifying streams wherever they can produce the richest results.

This, however, is only the first condition. If the right of national governments to create national armed forces no longer threatens the peace of the world as it does now, there still remains the second sovereign right to erect tariff barriers to be dealt with. I do not myself contemplate the complete abolition of all tariffs. They are, and are likely to remain, a convenient system for raising revenue to the extent to which they are not protective; they may also in certain cases be of use as a considered counterpart of general policy to secure certain social purposes. They may, for example, be deliberately used in some cases to prevent a given country being completely specialized upon one or two forms of economic activity, with the monotony of social life which that might cause. Australia, for example, might desire, at what she would recognize to be a definite cost, to secure the richer variety of national life that is open to a country with industrial as well as agricultural activities as compared with one which concentrates only upon the production of grain and raw materials.

But the great difference will be that world tariff policies will be reasonably stable, and will be a definite part of a considered policy, both national and international. It will be recognized that changes when they are required must be made after prolonged and careful discussion of the international consequences involved. In a word, future tariff commissions will not be just national but international. Those who are heard before a decision is taken will not be only the different classses of industrialists or consumers in a single country, but the representatives of all the countries on whom any proposed new tariff will react. The officials concerned will regard it as just as normal and inevitable a part of their procedure to discuss any proposed new policy with the corresponding officials of other countries, as they now do to discuss it with the representatives of other departments in a departmental committee in their own country. The specialized committees at Geneva which I have already described dealing with economic, financial, social, legal, colonial, and other questions will no longer be merely advisory bodies attempting with varying success to influence national governments to exercise the real power. They will be an integral and a central part of the real mechanism of the government of the world.

And then, at last, on a basis of secure confidence and peace, and of stability in commercial policy, the way will be clear for the world to devote its real efforts to achieve positive progress in civilization.

Let me give a few examples only of what can and should be done. The world's official government at Geneva, side by side with an enlarged and developed international bank, can give the world a stable and satisfactory currency system, an inestimable advantage for the development of world trade. It can similarly develop a code and a tradition for foreign lending (enforced where necessary by co-ordinated legal sanctions) which will stop reckless borrowing and irresponsible lending, will reduce the risk of loss to the investor, will prevent savings being wasted as they now are, and will direct them in fertilizing streams where they are most needed and will be most useful.

Upon such a securely established foundation of world government, man will at last be able to reap the fruits of nature's riches and of his own increasing skill and knowledge. The last quarter of a century has given us more power over nature than all the previous centuries of recorded history; the next quarter of a century may well do as much or more.

If these present and future resources of knowledge can be used in a world purged of war and of the fear of war, can find full scope in free and secure world markets aided by a single stable currency on a perfected credit system, the general standard of living can be increased beyond all present imagining. The world can establish a point beyond which individual luxury and extravagance shall not be allowed to pass, and a level below which individual human comfort shall not be allowed to fall; and this level can be such that every man will have both the necessities and the reasonable luxuries of life, and adequate leisure to enjoy all our rich heritage of culture and civilization.

INDEX

DATE DUE

GAYLORD			PRINTED IN U.S.A